When the Dust Rises

When the Dust Rises

An Anthology by
Mount Vernon Migrant Youth

Edited by Janice Blackmore,
Jennifer Morison Hendrix,
and Matt Malyon

Printed in 2019 by Village Books, Bellingham, Washington, in the United
States of America

ISBN 978-0-9996704-2-2
LCCN 2013919376

Cover design: Daniel Galán
Cover image: Ismael Angel Santana
Lead photographer: Alvin Shim

Contents

EL PESO DE LAS SOMBRAS 91

LOS CAMPOS 115

AFTERWORD 205

CREDITS 235
INDEX 237

Foreword

We Will Be Together Again

Celebrate these teen writers, sons and daughters. Celebrate them for their courage—for their almost impossible strength to continue, for their will to live.

Celebrate these young migrant youth for walking us through their life-struggles. To stay alive, to strive to keep their memories of their families whole, even though they have lived their days with families torn in pieces, thrown into the invisible realms of deportation, separation and loss.

These are words of truth, scenes of reality, word-fire from wounds, tears from days and years of split-family pain—and the sculpting of love, and the forging of will, and the building of friendship, and the revelations and strengthening of core spirit. Celebrate. These are much more than poets and writers—these youth leaders are our heart-teachers.

Our heart-teachers pick up the shards, the splinters, the never-mentioned invisibilized lives of our migrante families, documented and undocumented, papers or no papeles, and ink and splash them onto these pages for our soulful reflections. Every word is a healing word. Every word is an incredible word. Every word is a word from deep nights of aloneness and from the sun-blaze of blistering work and the feverish joy of creativity, reclaimed voice and sudden being.

Being? Yes—to finally arrive at one's true liberation in the midst of a life at the margins, exploited, unacknowledged and abandoned in this place called America. Celebrate being held up on their shoulders. If you do so, you will have touched their truth-power, you will have let their life-force enter your blood. You will see them face to face, at last. And then what?

The rest is up to you. You too will be whole. And we will be together again.

Juan Felipe Herrera
Son of migrant farmworkers
United States Poet Laureate (2015–2017)

Estaremos juntos otra vez

(Spanish version translated from English)
Honremos a estos jóvenes escritores, hijos e hijas—celebremos
su valentía—por su casi imposible fuerza para continuar, por su
voluntad de vivir.

Honremos a estos jóvenes migrantes por guiarnos a lo largo de
sus luchas en la vida. Por seguir vivos, por esforzarse por
mantener íntegras las memorias de sus familias, a pesar de que
han vivido sus días con familias partidas en pedazos, arrojados a
las invisibles realidades de la deportación, la separación y la
pérdida.

Estas palabras dicen la verdad, son escenas de la realidad,
palabras-fuego de las heridas, lágrimas de días y años de dolor de
la separación de familias—y la escultura del amor, y la forja de la
voluntad, y el construir de la amistad, y las revelaciones y
fortalecimiento del núcleo espiritual. Celebremos—estos son más
que poetas y escritores—estos líderes de la juventud son nuestro
corazón-maestros.

Nuestros maestros-corazón recogen los fragmentos, las astillas,
las nunca mencionadas e invisibilizadas vidas de nuestras familias
migrantes, documentadas e indocumentadas, con papeles o sin
papeles, y los lanzan con tinta en estas páginas para nuestras
sentidas reflexiónes. Cada palabra es una palabra de curación.
Cada palabra es una increíble palabra. Cada palabra es una palabra
que surge de las profundas noches de soledad y del fuego del
trabajo abrasador y el febril regocijo de la creatividad, voz
recuperada y repentino ser.

¿Ser? Sí—para llegar por fin a nuestra verdadera liberación enmedio de una vida en las márgenes, explotados, sin ser reconocidos y abandonados en este lugar llamado América. Celebremos ser sostenidos sobre sus hombros. Si así lo hacéis, habréis tocado su poder-de-la-verdad, habréis dejado entrar en su sangre la fuerza de vida. Los veréis cara a cara, por fin. ¿Y después, qué?

El resto lo deciden ustedes. Ustedes también estarán enteros. Y todos estaremos juntos otra vez.

Juan Felipe Herrera
Hijo de trabajadores agrícolas migrantes
Poeta Laureado de los Estados Unidos

Lauro Flores
Traductor, Universidad de Washington, Seattle, Washington

"I know where we're going
Where we always go
To some detention center to some fingerprinting hall or cube
Some warehouse warehouse after warehouse"
          "Borderbus" by Juan Felipe Herrara *

"I was there on my momma's back,
two years old,
feet dangling from the rebozo…"
          "I Am an Immigrant" by Rocio

"Home isn't home
If you can't stay
Home isn't home
If it has to be this way."
          "Justice for All" by Azucena

* Excerpt from "Border Bus" by Juan Felipe Herrera, from *Notes on the Assemblage* © 2015, reprinted with permission of City Lights Books, www.citylights.com.

Going Back

"The Desert Goes On Forever When You're Walking"

Fuego Nuevo

Immigration is a hotly debated topic in the United States, and most people assume that it is only a political or economic issue. For families coming from Latin America, though, where unemployment and crime rates are high, immigration is also a spiritual issue. It is about leaving a place of hopelessness and risking everything for a new start. Like the religious ceremonies celebrated by the ancient Aztecs, immigrants sacrifice everything to mark the beginning of a new life.

The pre-Hispanic Aztecs used two calendars—a solar calendar based on astronomy and a religious calendar. Together, these two calendars rolled through time like giant intersecting wheels that completed a great cycle once every 52 solar years. At that pivotal moment, the Aztec people performed the ritual of Fuego Neuvo, or New Fire, to restore balance in the universe and signify a new beginning.

First, they extinguished all the fires so that cities were left in total darkness. At sunset, the clergy started walking solemnly to a hill called Huixachtecatl, which was in Iztapalapa (ancient Culhua city in the southern part of Lake Texcoco). Huixachtecatl means Cerro de la Estrella (Hill of the Star) because that night their attention was fixed on the firmament.

During the journey to Iztapalapa, the priests made sporadic stops to light small bonfires as a test. Meanwhile, the people waited on the roofs of their houses, expectant and practicing their own rites. They fasted for five days before the ceremony and ate only tzohuatl, which is amaranth with honey, and did not drink anything until noon. Pregnant women wore masks of maguey to prevent the darkness from becoming tzitzimime (skeleton-like deities that appeared in moments of disaster, such as earthquakes; the Spaniards considered them demons). They kept their children awake, also masked, so they did not turn into mice.

The procession to the top of Huixachtecatl lasted about six hours. When the Tianquiztli (Pleiades) were in the right position, around midnight, a priest lit a large fire on the terrace of the Teocalli (a temple). If the flames were maintained, the continuity of the world was ensured. When the pyre was big enough and the Anahuac Valley was completely dark, the light was visible at a great distance, and everyone knew they were safe.

Before celebrating the beginning of a new cycle, it was also necessary to show penance. All the people would prick their ears with cactus thorns, children and babies, too, until they bled. Then came the time to get rid of material goods so that the people could be completely renewed. Everything was destroyed, even statuettes of their gods, and the priests in the temples replaced the old statues with new ones. Whatever could not be burned was thrown into the ditches or the bottom of the lake. Heralds carried torches lit from the New Fire to temples throughout the region, and all the neighbors lit torches to light their own homes. Sadness and fear turned into joy, with dancing and music.

Fuego Nuevo is reflected in the lives of many immigrants, who leave everything behind in order to flee a corrupt environment and raise their children in a better place. Fuego Neuvo represents the ambition and determination of migrant workers, who accept the fear of deportation as a penance but at the same time look forward to a new future, where their children will not have to worry about whether they will survive the night.

Adrian, 17 years old

I Am an Immigrant

Being an immigrant, it's always so great…

1

I love my family, I mean really, who wouldn't.
It's so huge, and awesome,
and all the parties we have!
Don't even get me started,
I could go on, and on, and on…

Actually, I hate it.

It's like,
I just…
automatically become an impassive person,
because that's **not** MY family.

In MY family we are **constantly** reminded
that we have no papers,
so every time someone speaks about us, all **we** can do
is lie back and listen…

2

Everybody loves it when I speak Spanish.
Yeah…

NO.

As soon as someone figures out my mom can't speak English,
they decide they're no longer able to serve her.
Isn't that crazy?
Nope.
I mean,

it's expected when it happens to you so often. Right?
That's why I always felt embarrassed of my mom
whenever I walked into a store with her.
I should be embarrassed of **myself**.
I can't even speak my own native tongue—
not Spanish, I couldn't care less for that language.
I mean Mixteco, which I have slowly killed
through my ignorance.
I am ashamed…

3

I'm so lucky I have brown skin.
Isn't everyone trying to get that tan?
Yeah…
I don't count.

Last time I checked, my skin was
too ashy,
too just-not-right.
My skin makes it obvious that I don't fit in,
that at any moment, anyone could ask me,
"Do you have papers?"
and I,
I won't be able to respond.
MLK, looks like my skin **still** defines me.

4

I am diverse.
I've got those **strong** genes.
My genes are powerful.
They trumped natural selection.
And I am a minority,
as in people with minor representation.
It's not a bad thing,

but why is it that
every time I turn the TV on,
we are the subject of discussion?

Like, "Mr. President, what are you gonna do
about the **illegal** immigrants in the country?"
Huh…
Just had to make that clear, we're **illegal**.
They hate it when we overlook that fact or "fail" to recognize it.
Hey, I didn't,
Because **I get it**.

I now know that when people hear "immigrant," they imagine
criminals,
ill-mannered
people with no class,
illegal aliens.
Huh…
I mean, it's not like we even own any UFOs!

5

I have a secret.
Shhhhh…
Don't tell anyone.
I
have
super powers!
Yeah, you heard right.
I have super powers.
I am invisible!
But somehow…
every time I enter a room, it follows me,
the fact that I am an immigrant.
In elementary,

kids used to be like, "La migra!"
It was a joke!
But they had **no** right,
and we,
we have no rights.

I was there on my momma's back,
two years old,
feet dangling from the rebozo,
feet turning black, yellow, and blue.
We didn't cross the border, the border crossed us.
Wrong!
We crossed that border,
and it was because of a dream and hope.
Yes,
I will continue to follow that dream.
We have **reasons**, people just can't understand that.

Sir, I want you to know,
there was more to me at two years of my life
than you will ever have in your whole existence.
I hold that to be self-evident.

Please don't be offended, this is all my opinion
There's nothing **I'm** saying wrong. *

Rocio, 14 years old
Monologue from 2017 production of *The Hidden Truth: Untold Stories*

* Final two lines inspired by "Video," a song by India.Arie

Understand Me

Ms. Jones? You wanted to know why my paper is late?

I'll tell you something that not everyone knows about me, why I'm different from my classmates, why sometimes I'm really shy and why I feel that nadie me entenderá. I'm 18 years old. I lived in Oaxaca for seven years with my mom. I came to Mount Vernon on August 22, 2016. You should listen to my story.

This isn't the first time I have lived in Mount Vernon. My parents are immigrants. They came here in 1998 to have a better life and more opportunities, but they didn't know that it would be so hard.

I was born in Lincoln City, Oregon. When I was two years old, my parents came to Mount Vernon, Washington. I lived here for six years, but my parents always worked. They didn't have time to stay at home with me. I grew up with a babysitter. I spoke a little bit of Spanish at home, but I spoke English at school and with my babysitter. Then my parents split up.

My mom thought that living here would be difficult with four children because she would have to work all the time so she could have money to pay the rent and bills. So, she took us back to Oaxaca when I was eight years old. I lived for the next seven years in Tlaxiaco, with my mom, my two sisters, and my brother. I'm the oldest, so I had to be an example for them.

When we lived in Mexico, I also had to take care of my siblings because my dad lost his job in 2010. My mom had to work to get money so my siblings and I would have something to eat. I had trouble when I first arrived in Mexico because I didn't speak

Spanish and some kids bullied me. They thought I was too stuck up to talk with them. Within two years, I had learned to speak Spanish, but I didn't practice my English, so now I am having to learn English again.

Are you beginning to understand?

In Mexico everything was different. I don't have Mexican papers because I wasn't born there, so I didn't have many opportunities. I had to pay to go to the doctor, and I didn't qualify for the school scholarships. I finished elementary school in 2013 and started middle school, but it was so expensive because I needed to buy everything. I finished middle school in 2015, and I wanted to continue my studies, but I couldn't do it in Mexico because I didn't have papers. I'm a US citizen. So, I decided to come here and live with my dad so I could go to high school.

I took the plane from Mexico to Tijuana and my uncle picked me up at the airport. My dad was waiting for me in Madera, California—he was afraid to go closer to the border.

Last year I wanted to go to Mexico so I could see my mom and siblings. My dad didn't have the money to buy the plane ticket, so I started working in the fields to get money to buy my ticket Working in the fields was difficult. It was so cold in the mornings and so hot in the afternoons, and I saw how Mexican people need to work very hard to have money and to take care of their children.

Living here with only my dad sometimes makes me feel very sad because he always is working. He doesn't have time to stay at home with me or to talk about school. He is always tired. When he gets to my house, he only takes a shower and eats and then goes to sleep so he can get up the next morning and go to work again. He is trying to give me and my siblings a better future.

So maybe now you understand why sometimes I take more time to do things in class. I'm not going anywhere. I will continue studying at Mount Vernon High School and do my best because I want to pass all my classes with good grades. And I want my parents to feel proud and see that everything they have done, all the fatigue, was worth it.

Litzy, 18 years old
Monologue from 2019 production of
The Hidden Truth: Breaking the Wall

You Think You Know Me?

You think you know me? Really? Sure, some of you have known me since kindergarten. But there's a lot you don't know about me. And no, I'm not talking about boy problems.

I was born in November 2003 in Mount Vernon, Washington. After three years, I went to Mexico with my one-year-old sister and my parents and started school in Oaxaca. I was bullied because I couldn't speak the native language even though my parents spoke Mixteco and Trique.

After six months my parents told me they were going to go away for a while. I didn't know they were going to cross the border and go back to Washington.

Months passed. I was at my grandparents' house one weekend. On the weekends we usually went to the big city to buy food, but this time it was different. We stopped by the side of the road, and I saw a woman get out of a yellow cab. It was Dania—my babysitter from Washington.

My aunt told me Dania was going to take my sister and me to my parents. My uncle had to drag us to the cab. We drove for hours. My little sister wouldn't stop crying until we stopped and got her a Coca-Cola. I remember being in the airplane and looking down on some big city with tall buildings.

I also remember when we got to Dania's daycare in Mount Vernon. My sister and I were settled on the floor, ready to go to sleep, when my parents came at 10:14 p.m. I'm pretty sure my mom started to cry because when I hugged her, her face was wet.

We lived with two uncles, two aunts, two cousins, and my cousins' grandma in a two-bedroom apartment for almost a year. One night I was watching TV downstairs when we heard screams and loud noises. We went up and opened the door to one of the bedrooms and saw that my aunt and uncle were fighting. Their noses were bloody.

My uncle wanted to go to his mother's funeral in Mexico, but my aunt didn't want him to go. She was pregnant, and she was afraid he'd have trouble crossing the border. In the end he decided to go. He never came back.

Nine months later, I finally got to go to school. I was bullied during kindergarten and first grade mostly because I couldn't speak the native language. I've always had good friends along the way. In the third grade I was really comfortable with my friends and would speak my mind, unless the teacher was close by.

My summers always consisted of babysitting my siblings. It was awful. I felt isolated and it wasn't much fun, considering we didn't have much to do, other than watch TV and clean. That's why I never looked forward to the end of the school year. Although last summer was the hardest. My family got evicted, and we had nowhere to go. We ended up staying in a motel.

Where do you spend your summers?

So next time you meet me in the hall and see the smile on my face or laugh at my jokes, maybe you should look again. And remember that everyone is dragging an invisible past behind them.

Yaneyda, 15 years old
Monologue from 2019 production of
The Hidden Truth: Breaking the Wall

Going Back

I had barely turned six when my parents made a decision that would change my life. It was March of 2008 when we started to pack up. I did not really know what was going on. I remember perfectly that it was night when we left. We were leaving the only home I had ever known: Everett, Washington.

Our journey was about eight days long; we had moved to Tepic, Nayarit, Mexico. You are probably wondering why we moved to Mexico. The main reason is because my dad's parents were in a car crash. My grandfather died, and my grandmother got severely injured. My dad had to take care of her, but he did not want to leave us alone in Washington. So, he took us with him.

I used to speak English and a little bit of Spanish, so guess what? I had to learn Spanish! As the years passed, I was learning Spanish very well, but at the same time I was forgetting how to speak English. One time my mom asked me, "Do you like Mexico?" I answered, "No, mom, not at all." I didn't see Mexico as my home. Thankfully, my grandmother got better after a couple of years, and she is currently doing fine.

In Mexico, I did great at school. In elementary school, I was known for being pretty intelligent. I participated in the National Olympics of Mathematics. I did not win, but it was an awesome experience. In middle school, I was the smartest. I was a great student model for my classmates. All the teachers recognized me as a leader.

However, in the summer of 2015, I was sad to learn that my parents had decided to return to the United States. I knew that all the success that I had shaped in Mexico was going to fall apart. I was frustrated that we were going to have to start all over again, but it was not my decision.

After three months selling everything that we had in Mexico, we were ready to return…ready to live again in the US. I was worried that my English was going to be pretty bad, but it wasn't. I was really impressed with myself because I hadn't spoken English for a very long time, to be specific, for seven long years.

My parents enrolled me in LaVenture Middle School. I made friends who always supported me when I needed help, but now I am the one who helps them.

I am not who I am right now only because of me; I am who I am because of my parents, because of their support, because of the challenges that they have given me. I will be someone important to the world thanks to them. I could have chosen to avoid these challenges, but I wanted my parents to be proud of me. I am proud of them for always being there for me.

Adrian, 16 years old
Monologue from 2017 production of *The Hidden Truth: Untold Stories*

The Move

When I was in the fourth grade, my family was living with my grandma in Mount Vernon because my parents couldn't pay anymore for the house we used to have. One day, my older sisters and my little brother and I were all in school. When we got home, my dad wasn't there. My mom didn't tell my little brother and me anything, so we just thought he wasn't there. After a few days, she finally told us that he was going to get deported and that we were moving to Mexico to be with him.

I felt sad and mad because we were going to have to leave all of our family and everything behind. I wouldn't be at school anymore, and we were going to have to leave my older sisters here in Mount Vernon to finish out the school year. I felt sad that my dad was getting deported because he also had to just leave suddenly. He wasn't in Mexico yet—they left him in detention in Tacoma. We went to see him twice and it was good to see him, but he looked really sad.

My dad was finally deported to Guadalajara, because that's where he was born, but then he got on a plane to Tijuana because it was closer to the border. He wanted us to go to school in the US. My dad got to Tijuana, Mexico, a little bit before us. He was staying with one of his friends, so we all stayed there for a couple of months. Then we got a house. My mom got a job at Kmart across the border in Chula Vista. My dad started selling clothes at a tíanguis (an outdoor market).

Every day I woke up about 4:30 a.m., got ready, and drove to the border about 5:30 a.m. The border wait was sometimes so long, it took us a few hours to get across. Once we were in the US, it was about five minutes to get to our school. My brother went to a different school, and our schools started at the same time, so often one of us was on time, but one of us was late. Our car had a lot of mechanical problems so sometimes it would die in the line at the border, and I wouldn't make it to school. That happened three or four times.

I got to school late. **A lot.** I was also absent a lot, sometimes because of car trouble, and sometimes because my mom was really tired, and sometimes because we had family conflicts. My teacher yelled at me almost every time I was late. She would say, "You are always late. I looked at your record from when you were in Washington, and it said you were always late and always absent." This just wasn't true! Then she would start to teach a lesson, but I would be crying still from when she yelled at me. I would feel mad because I always did really well in school and, at that school, I was doing really bad, and I wasn't used to that.

About half way through the year, I was missing a lot of school because of really bad family problems. Then I was absent for a while because my aunt died, and my family traveled to where she lived two hours away. Afterward we tried to give the teacher a note about what happened, but she didn't believe me. Then I found out that when I was absent, staff from the school went to the address my mom had given them, but it wasn't my real address. It wasn't where I lived. The people who did live there told them I lived in Mexico. Since you can't go to school in California if you live in Mexico, they kicked me out. I never got my stuff from the classroom because my mom was mad and didn't want me to go back to that school.

Linda, 11 years old

Dos veces migrante

(English translation follows)
Yo he sido dos veces migrante
Y ambas no fue mi elección
Es difícil ser nueva en la escuela
Y mucho más si es por migración
Es complicado no entender el idioma
Que se habla en esta nueva nación

Porque son varias las razones
Que llevan a las personas a tomar esta decisión
Una de ellas es el ir en busca
De para su familia un futuro mejor
El dejar parte de la familia en México
Créanme ha causado un gran dolor

Yo soy hija de mexicanos
Que por razones del destino un día se juntaron
Tuvieron hijos, un hogar, un trabajo,
Pero de repente un día se separaron
Esa fue la primera vez que emigre
Y así fue como con mi madre y mis hermanos a México viaje

Fue un viaje complicado por el que pase
Vi a mis hermanos y a mi madre complicaciones tener
En el camino a este nuevo hogar
Había aún muchas lágrimas por caer
Para los que no conocíamos, un nuevo idioma,
Un nuevo país, una nueva cultura había por entender

Llevo un poco de tiempo, pero me acostumbre
Mi primaria y secundaria en México estudié

Hace unos pocos meses a México regrese
Pero no como hubiese querido porque del inglés me olvide
Aunque sé que con el tiempo nuevamente lo aprenderé

Ahora que volví a Mount Vernon
Después de casi 10 años a mi padre volví a ver
Fueron bonitos los sentimientos que había por remover
Aunque para ello a mi madre y hermana menos en México deje
Y es así como les cuento las dos veces
Que por circunstancias distintas emigre.

Juliana, 16 years old
Spoken word poem from 2019 production of
The Hidden Truth: Breaking the Wall

Twice a Migrant

(translated from Spanish)

I have been a migrant twice
and both times weren't my choice.
It's difficult to be new in school,
and even more if it's because of migration.
It's complicated to not understand the language
spoken in this new nation.

There are various reasons
why a person makes this decision,
and one of them is so they can go in search
of a better future for their family.
Leaving part of the family in Mexico,
believe me, has caused real pain.
I am the daughter of Mexican parents
who met because of destiny.
They had kids, a home, work,
but suddenly one day they separated.
That was the first time I migrated
and that's why my mother, my siblings, and I traveled to Mexico.

It was a difficult trip.
I saw my siblings and mother have complications
along the way to this new home.
There were many tears shed,
for the new people we hadn't met,
a new language, a new country, a new culture that we had to
understand.

A little time passed, and I got used to it all.
My elementary and middle school years I spent in Mexico.

A few months ago, I returned to the US,
but not like I had wanted,
because I had forgotten my English,
although I know with time, I will learn it again.

Now that I am back in Mount Vernon,
after almost ten years, I finally saw my dad again.
Many beautiful, hidden feelings were revealed,
although for him I had to leave my mother and sister.
And that is the story of how twice,
for distinct reasons, I immigrated.

Juliana, 16 years old

Foreign National

I've aged a bit, and they said I'd know more, but they never told me I would also forget. At five, I promised myself I was meant for more than this world could offer. Now I'm 16, and I sometimes doubt I should have a place in this world.

I'll be a senior next year, one more school year left before graduation. Mount Vernon, Washington, has been the raising ground of migrant kids like me, exactly like me, most especially me. The accessibility to the Migrant Leaders Club has given me an outlet to confidently speak and be heard. How cliché that must sound, but, with a lack of words, it's sometimes the easiest and most truthful phrase to voice.

I haven't made that little five-year-old girl proud, the child of her mother, indigenous from her roots to the clouds. That little girl said:

If I were in charge of the world, there would be music on the street and food everywhere, so people could eat, dance, and drink.

If I were in charge of the world,
you wouldn't have "sad,"
you wouldn't have "dirty,"
you wouldn't have puberty or sickness,
you wouldn't even have "I told you so."

Rocio, 16 years old

This Is Me

My name is Brianna. I am the granddaughter of Felicitas and Eusebio and Carolina and Jorge—Latinx on both sides.

In the 1960s my mother's grandfather Ruben was a bracero, a farmworker who traveled from Mexico to the United States to work in the fields. He traveled to work for many months, leaving my great abuela alone with the children in Mexico. This went on for many years. Eventually his wife and their first three daughters, including my grandmother, traveled with him. They were braceros, too, working very long days in the heat of California for little money.

My great grandparents had a total of 12 kids, and the travel between countries went on for more than 25 years. All of their kids were born in Mexico. Because the family was living in Baja California, they crossed the border on a daily basis, so some of the next generation were born in the United States and became legal residents.

My great grandparents never had the opportunity to attend school. They worked and raised their kids. Great abuelo did manage to learn to read and write at church, but my great abuela never did. My grandmother, Felicitas, had to leave school after the second grade because she helped with raising the kids. Great abuelo died in his early 70s from a heart attack. Great grandma Ludivina is still alive and is a big part of our family.

My family worked hard in the fields and factories for many years at very low pay. They worked in the tulips, potatoes, cucumbers, strawberries, and raspberries. They sent their kids to school every day. The kids also worked the fields but only in the summer.

Most married couples and their children migrated together with the great abuelos. While they lived in several areas of California, eventually most followed to Washington. The younger ones, now my mother and aunts, had a very hard time moving because they had to leave their friends behind. My grandmother Felicitas died at the young age of 40 from cancer—probably from exposure to chemicals while she was in the fields.

I have had a privileged life. My family are fair-skinned people, even the braceros. We got bullied less and were given more opportunities. This does not mean we did not suffer trauma as migrants or worry about deportation. Some in my family did get deported. Some children were separated from their parents. Some of my older cousins were terrified and worried for many years that they would come home and find their parents ... just gone.

Some in my family were victims of the broken immigration system and had to wait more than 20 years to get their green cards even though they were eligible, applied, and paid their fees. And it matters—not having a green card. It makes you vulnerable to powerful institutions.

Because of my family's story, I am interested in helping my migrant friends. I want to use my privilege to help others that don't have it. In my opinion, migrants are wise. They are grateful, and they appreciate every little thing they get. I learn a lot from their experience, and it helps me remember where my family came from.

So, you understand why I might get very offended when Trump calls Mexicans drug dealers and criminals. In fact, the migrants that I know work harder to earn a living than a lot of the citizens I know.

The United States was a land of First Nations people. It was the colonizers who left their countries seeking a better life here. They were the ones who brought slaves and encouraged immigration. The people who are privileged now? They made this a nation of immigrants.

Now we need to be a nation that welcomes those who pick our crops and put food on the table for us. Maybe I should be the president of the United States one day so I can make sure people feel welcome.

Brianna, 12 years old
Monologue from 2019 production of
The Hidden Truth: Breaking the Wall

Generations

Azucena's mother (second from right) with her mother
and siblings in Oaxaca, Mexico

Marcela's parents in the tulip fields, Skagit County, Washington
Photograph by Moises, their son

"Mi piel, muy mexicana, oaxaqueña y muy humana. Del color de mi tierra y la diversidad de sus colores."
    Yalitza Aparicio

"I am from the coughing of the chile
        burning on the comal
The 'xindá'ví-iniún' and 'kuákusou'
The killing chickens
And 'vamos a hacer tortillas'"
    "Where I Am From" by Nayeli

"Every morning, when I was a little girl, I would wake up between my mom, saying 'nana,' and dad, saying 'tata,' and tell them, 'Di'i ku ña' (it's sunny), and every night I would say, 'Nu'u ku ña' (it's night)."
    "Tata" by Eloisa

Este soy yo

Photograph by Alfonso

Where I Am From

I am from the handmade mandil
The 3 sacks of flour
Religious altars
And old pictures on the wall

I am from the 6 cars in the parking space
The tomatoes
My mom's flowers
And cilantro
Growing in my mom's favorite place

I am from the family of 10
Nayeli
Francisca
Luis
Cresencio
Raul
Antonia
Federico
Lionel
Fredy
And Floresita

I am from the coughing of the chile burning on the comal
The "xindá'ví-iniún" and "kuákusou"
The killing chickens
And "vamos a hacer tortillas"

I am in love with enchiladas
Spicy red molé
Tacos de asada

Arroz con leche
And warm tortillas

I am from the fields
The "levantate, ya es hora" at 5 a.m.
Dirty hands and clothes
I am the sweat of the summer sun
And los campos, where we used to go

I am from the indigenous Mixteco language
The respect
Hard work
And religious beliefs

I am from bautismos
Día de los Muertos
And traditional dances

I am from the parents of Santa Catarina Noltepec

Nayeli, 15 years old

<table>
<tr><td colspan="2" align="center">Glossary</td></tr>
<tr><td>mandil</td><td>apron (Spanish)</td></tr>
<tr><td>xindá'ví-iniún</td><td>thank you (Mixteco)</td></tr>
<tr><td>kuákusou</td><td>go to sleep (Mixteco)</td></tr>
<tr><td>vamos a hacer tortillas</td><td>we are going to make tortillas (Spanish)</td></tr>
<tr><td>levántate, ya es hora</td><td>wake up, it's time (Spanish)</td></tr>
<tr><td>los campos</td><td>camps for migrant workers (Spanglish)</td></tr>
<tr><td>bautismos</td><td>baptisms (Spanish)</td></tr>
<tr><td>Día de los Muertos</td><td>Day of the Dead (Spanish)</td></tr>
</table>

Nayeli exploring her parents' hometown in Oaxaca, Mexico
Photograph by her sister, Floresita

Tata

As a kid, I was born with two parents, how most kids are born. I was quite chubby as a little girl, adorable is what they would call me, and I was quiet and calm. I was the youngest in my family of seven, now known as a family of six.

Since I was the youngest in the family, my parents put their attention mainly on me. Every morning, when I was a little girl, I would wake up between my mom, saying "nana," and my dad, saying "tata," and tell them, "Di'i ku ña" (it's sunny), and every night I would say, "Nu'u ku ña" (it's night).

When I was younger, I viewed the world differently than how I view it now. My sisters taught me how to speak English when I was about five, and they taught me to count. To me, I thought the highest number was 100. This made me think the world only contained 100 people, my family, my community and the place where I lived. I didn't think of different races or even know what a race was. I didn't know that humans could be illegal, that there were such things as borders. Even if I had known what these words meant, they wouldn't have bothered my five-year-old self.

At that time, my dad would call me all sorts of names, tiquañu (squirrel), oso (bear), and nana leso (the mother of bunnies). He would always make me laugh with all the jokes he would tell the family. Whenever I came home, my dad would tell me to kiss him on the cheek, and I would because I really loved him.

I lived in a tall, pale pink house. There were three dark rooms and a bathroom in the basement of the house. I remember I accidentally locked myself in the bathroom, and I cried because I couldn't reach the lock. My brother had to go around the house, open the window, and help me out. Upstairs was the living room and kitchen, and it was usually brighter up there. That was where I would spend most of my time, playing with my cousin and my sister. There was a door that led outside to a porch. I remember my brother telling my sister, "You wanna see me jump off this porch?" She told him it wasn't a good idea, but he went for it anyway. When he jumped off, he hit the ground hard, landing on his stomach.

I didn't have many cousins to play with since they were either too far away or older than me. I only had one cousin who would come over and visit. She was a year younger than me, and she was my best friend. I would always talk to her about school and other stuff. We would turn on music and dance together. My older sister was also my best friend. I would hang out with her every single day. We would play with the stuffed animals I owned. She was there for me when I was sent to the hospital because my stomach was hurting from a blockage. My sister was also there for me whenever I would cry, but she never told me about the things that were happening to her. She had her own secret that I wish I had known earlier.

I have another older sister and two older brothers. When I was younger, I don't know why, but I never really interacted with them. It was like they were strangers to me. My second brother was kind to me, but I never knew who he truly was. My older sister didn't tell me anything that was going on, probably because I was the youngest, and she felt like there was no need. I was the only one who didn't have to go through the pain they went through. I was the only one who didn't have to face the deep truth of abuse.

My aunt was my favorite person at that time. I would always be jealous when she would talk to other young girls. But I didn't know what she was going through either. I couldn't see the pain she was hiding. Whenever I would cry, she would always be there to tell me to stop crying. I would always believe her when she would say, "Ela, stop crying. If you cry more, you're wasting your blood. Your tears are your blood." I remember one day, I saw her standing in the kitchen. She took out a knife from the drawer and pointed it at her stomach. I didn't understand anything that was going on. I saw her talking to herself and standing in that same position for a long time. She didn't hurt herself, but in her mind, she wanted to.

In school, I had friends of my own, too. I would always make friends. Back then I was more active, happier, and I didn't care what anyone would think. I had one friend that would always make me wonder. When it was sunny, we both would lie under the trees and look at the clouds to see what shapes they would make. She spoke her mind, and I had fun with her every day in school. But when I would go home, it was different. Sometimes my dad would suddenly not be home anymore. I wasn't worried that much because I never really knew what was happening. I never really knew the police would always come to take him away. I distinctly remember my mom was braiding my hair and my sister's hair, and I saw my dad come up the stairs. I was happy; he had been gone for a long time, and I hadn't known why.

One day, my cousin, my sister, and I sat on the floor reading a book by the window upstairs in the pink house. It was quiet until a rock came flying through the window above us, then more rocks. My aunt yelled, "Stay away from the window!" and we immediately ran to the opposite side of the room. Glass was shattered everywhere, and rocks where inside the house. There was this girl outside who didn't like us, especially my brother. I remember that my aunt was hit in the head with a rock when she went outside to confront the girl, and the police came.

Starting in the summer when I was seven, certain days I would go along with my siblings and my parents to work in the fields, and some days I would stay home alone and do chores. When I went to the fields, they would hide me in the car. There were clothes and blankets inside that I would use to cover the windows, just in case the owners saw me. My sister would always come and check on me, but most of the time I was in the car alone. It would always be hot, and I would always be bored. Sometimes I would help my family out, but I always had to hide in the bushes. Then came the time I was old enough to work. I was about ten, and I would work every day in the summers and not take any breaks.

Then the summer of 2013 came, the last summer I would spend with my father. He was kind in every way, he would help people on the streets, he would make many friends, and some would even give him discounts. Overall, he was a loving father, but when I was little, he was different. He would drink a lot and would fight with my mom. They would always argue, even in front of my sisters and me. I would always cry whenever I saw this happening.

Their fighting was a very specific sound that I can't explain but that I remember really well. Their fighting gave me trauma. One time it got even worse, when he went to the kitchen and grabbed a knife. My mom was the one who told us to get in the car. He came running with the knife, but before he could make it to the car, my mom drove off. We stopped by the park and spent the night sleeping in the car. We came back home in the morning.

When we started going to church, my father was baptized and chose to change his actions. Ever since that day, he tried to be a better father. He would take us on car trips. Once he drove the whole family to Cranberry Lake. He grilled meat while my sister and I played by the lake. My grandma, aunt, uncle, and parents were all there, and no one knew that this would be our last family vacation.

We didn't get summer vacations because we spent summers working in the fields. My mom was the one who was struggling the most. She worked by herself in a heavy-working job and would always work 14 hours a day. Sometimes she would leave in the morning, and sometimes in the night. She didn't have a job that most people would have. You might be thinking of a job in an office or something, but no. My mother worked for a seafood company where she would get on a small boat, then stop in the low tides to get out of the boat and dig for clams. The clams would be put in black crates, and the workers were paid by the pound. Every time she came home, I would always run to her and hug her. I could smell the faintly scented clams on her chaleco and the dry dirt on her clothes. She is the most special person in my heart, and I wouldn't be living if she wasn't here.

I also have a grandma, my father's mom, who I feel has been struggling, too. Whenever I come to visit my grandma, I always hold my tears inside because when I see her, she makes me feel sad. I would define my grandma as sweet, caring, strong, and with a good sense of humor. I want to cry in front of her, but I can't because I don't want her to see me crying. She has been through a lot, and I have always been the one seeing her cry. Her daughter, my aunt, recently got cancer but is now recovering and doing well. My aunt is the only person that is able to help my grandma, for my grandma still hasn't paid all her debt.

When my brother got into a car crash, the police called us and informed us. My mom then told my sisters and me, and then called my grandma. We were all crying. We were scared because he was sent to the hospital, and they said he would've died if he hadn't worn his seat belt. This happened during the night. They all drove off to the hospital in Bellingham to see him, except me. I have asked myself, "Why didn't I go?" I didn't go partly because I needed to go to sleep, but also because of him.

My second brother grew up being the opposite of my first brother. He would always get into fights with my older sister. There was one time she locked herself in the bathroom for hours crying because of him. When our family moved to the apartment, I remember hearing a knock on the door. During that time, I was doing my homework with my sister. When we heard a knock on the door, we told our brother to get the door since he was the oldest in the house at that time. He opened the door and a police officer was there looking for him. The police officer told him, "Come with me," and they left. When my mom came home from work, we told her that my brother had left with a police officer and still hadn't come home. My mom soon knew why he was taken, but I didn't know until my sister told me why.

After he got out of jail, he wasn't allowed to live with us for a while and lived with my mom's friend. When he was allowed to come home, he wasn't any different. He had a short temper and would always be mad for no reason. He spent time with grandpa, who was a bad influence. My grandpa is my dad's dad. He's always been an alcoholic and still is. He used to live with our family, but my mom didn't want him to live with us any longer and kicked him out because of his actions. I still see my grandpa in the streets, but we avoid him. I know he knows about my dad, his own son, but I feel like he had no emotions when he heard the news.

When we heard that my father had died, it was a depressing time. I didn't say this earlier, but my father was deported a lot. The last time he was sent to Mexico, he was told to stay there and that if he ever tried to come back, they would lock him up and not let him out. I never knew about deportation. When I would be told he was in jail, going to jail for being an immigrant never came to my mind. The only thing that I knew would send someone to jail was if you stole something. My younger self thought that if my dad had gone to jail, it must have been because he had stolen something, but that was not the answer.

The police came looking for him early in the morning one summer day and even threatened my brother to spit the truth out. Once he did, they took my father while he was trying to escape and sent him off to Mexico, far away from our family.

When we heard my father died, my brother cried in his room for days. My grandma was the one I felt most sad for because she had lost her oldest son, and her youngest son has never really recovered.

As days pass, a piece of my heart is still broken. It's empty. I try not to cry because I know it would hurt my father if I'm sad. My brother asks me "Why don't you ever feel sad that dad died?" I answer, "Just because I don't show it doesn't mean that I'm not sad."

I am who I am now because of my father. He taught me to be happy and make others happy, and I'm trying. He told me to be strong, that I should be grateful for what I have, and I am. Even though he's not here, I am grateful for a mom and for sisters that stay by my side even though I may be a struggle for them. I might not have a family like others, but the one I have is enough.

Even though I can't see you still, father, hopefully you can still see me. Even though I cry, I'm still happy that I was able to spend my childhood with you. I will always have a missing piece in my heart, and the only person that can fill it is you, tata.

Eloisa, 14 years old
Monologue from 2018 production of
The Hidden Truth: Unmasked

Mama

I love you, mama
I'm 16 years old
don't need my mom
driving on my own
going home early after work
this life is weird
this life
I feel good working hard for my sisters
I love you, mama
I do this for you, mama
I know he left you, mama
I can feel your pain
we did everything we could, mama
I know you can't understand
I say kotoi yo'o (I love you)
kundyai yo'o (I will take care of you)
ko'i shi'o, mama (I will live with you)
I would buy what you want, mama
I love you
I go to work at 6:00 a.m., mama
get out the next day at 4:00 a.m., mama
getting two hours of sleep, mama
I will always love you, mama.

Juan, 16 years old

Letter to My Mom

Mom, I know what you've done is for my own good as you say
but today I view things in a different way
You made me a reason to stay with the man
who brought you pain since he walked into your life
Since then I have seen myself as the knot in your string
and the reason you strive
I've built myself off anger to be strong for you
and to one day fight for you
But as the years have passed us, I learned
it was much more than me that stopped you from leaving
It's the love you have for that man that leads you on still grieving
Mom, I was lonely at one point in my life
when you sided with him
Right then I thought my chances of succeeding
were getting pretty slim
I was stuck in a tunnel with barely any light
I was fighting myself living wrong doing right
Mom, I don't blame you for how our life turned out to be
I know you nurtured and cried many tears for me
I apologize for leaving for days
without letting you know I was okay
But I needed that break to keep myself sane
See, when I was home, the air I'd breathe felt toxic
When you'd leave me with him
I spent hours sitting in that closet anxiously
Home no longer felt like home it felt like a gas chamber
It's the moments I escaped to be outside that I still savor
I couldn't fake a smile like you asked me to do
And I couldn't play the perfect daughter role
that you wanted me to
I did graduate school and accomplished many of the things

he swore I wouldn't
I got myself into some trouble and got myself out
when he thought that I couldn't
Every time I felt like I'd hit the dirt, I'd think about all the hurt
I reran the scene
when that man knocked me down and beat me on the floor
And that night I ran downstairs to you
when I didn't want him to touch me anymore
I feed my pride remembering
how I finally swung back to stop another attack
It still stings to remember what happened after that
But mom I still don't blame you for all of this
you went above and beyond to be a great mother
I promised myself to help you
recover all the happiness you deserve
And I hope you take the time to observe
that all the positive things I've done are dedicated to you
For soothing me during the rage
and getting me through the worst times of our lives
No more violence and no more tears in those big old eyes
I'll go outta my way to keep a smile on your face
Forever my mother, my hope and my faith
I'll love you forever and always
Sincerely, Tu Flaca

Yesica, 21 years old
Intern | Underground Writing
Writing mentor for Migrant Leaders Club,
2018–2019

The Story of My Birth

The story of my birth is scary.

When my mom was pregnant with me, she and my father were driving, and they got into a car crash. My mom fainted, and when she woke up, she had a tube down her throat, and she could not say anything.

When the nurse finally came to see her, the nurse said, "You have a baby boy!" Then my mom got stitches, and she named me Jesús.

Jesús, 12 years old

I'm a Fighter

I never met my biological father, but apparently, he was a drunk and he would hurt my family, and no one hurts my family.

I was born in Brawley, California; I moved to Somerton, Arizona, at the age of four. In Somerton, I felt like my life was complete. I had my group of friends. We were some smart kids, but we were also some big troublemakers. We would hang out every day without a miss. I thought my life was at its best and nothing could ruin it, until one horrible day.

When I was in the fifth grade, my little sister was hurt by a "man." It was so bad that she was sent to the E.R. I was furious. I told myself, "If I ever find him, he'll meet the devil face to face." We had to change the locks on the front door, and at night, I would get our biggest sofa and put it in front of the door and sleep there, even though I couldn't really sleep.

During this time, my mom was talking a lot with a guy in California named Felipe. They would talk on the phone for ages. Also, around this time, my mom met a lady visiting Arizona from Mount Vernon, Washington. This lady told my mom a lot about the place, and I guess my mom thought it sounded like a nice town. My mom told Felipe about Mount Vernon, and they thought it would be a good place to live because of the job opportunities.

Soon after, I saw my mom packing her stuff, and she told us to do the same. She said that we were moving. I felt my heart skip a beat. I didn't want to leave Somerton. I was mad and sad at the same time. When I told my pack that I was leaving, they were sad as well. The next day, they threw me a party. I felt happiness for the first time since my sister went to the hospital, but soon after we were gone, on our way to Washington.

When we got to Mount Vernon, I immediately wanted to go back to Somerton, but when I told my mom that I was going back no matter what, she knocked some sense into me, and I never mentioned wanting to go back again. We stayed with the lady my mom had met in Arizona until we finally got our own place.

But something was bugging me—Felipe. My mom married Felipe, and I didn't like it one bit. As time went by, I saw progressively worse things going on. Felipe was getting on my nerves. It's normal for a guy to act like the man of the house, but Felipe was acting like he was king of the damn city. For example, when he would be on the phone, we all had to be quiet or else. This made me mad every time. I felt like he needed to leave, or I would leave.

This past November, Felipe picked me up from school and took me to a burger shack, even though I wasn't hungry. When we sat down at the table, his eyes started to tear. He was very serious and said, "I'm going to ask you some questions." His first question was, "If I asked you to do something, would you do it?" I said, "It depends."

Then he gave me my mom's phone and asked me to unlock it, but I refused. I was considering grabbing my mom's phone and running home when he asked me his second question. "If the cops came and held me down, what would you do?" I said, "Investigate." He kept looking out the window; then he told me he was tired of everything and wanted to leave us. He told me we were having a conversation man to man, but I told him a real man doesn't give up at anything, especially family. I asked him,

"Do you want your young sons to be like me, hating every man who calls himself a "father"?

On December 2nd, not long after that conversation, Felipe left. I was mad and never wanted to see him again. I was glad he was gone, but it was hard to watch my mom suffer. It still makes me mad when I think about it.

You might be thinking that I'm a person that has experienced a lot of anger, but I want you to know that I have love all around me, people who care for me, and I protect them, too. I'll be a fighter until my last breath.

José, 16 years old
Monologue from 2017 production of *The Hidden Truth: Untold Stories*

The Truth Behind My Scars

Hey, I'm Javier. Who am I, you may ask? Let me tell you.

I'm a boy living in this gorgeous, not-so-gorgeous town. I'm a 16-year-old boy going to a multicultural school where I don't really fit in. I'm a little weird, a little awkward, a little short. Yeah, laugh if you want, but I really am 5 feet 4 inches. But that's not all about me; that is only the outside. You can only see my outside and never the inside. The outside only shows my scars, but on the inside they're still bleeding. These wounds are deep, deeper than anything, but I think they're beautiful. Yeah, they are in a way, at least to me, because they are what made me, me.

Let me tell you a bit more about myself. For many years, I had to go to daycare, up until I hit middle school. I remember waking up at five in the morning every day just to get dropped off with our care provider. I would stay there with two of my three little sisters for sometimes more than 12 hours a day. My care providers became a big influence in my life because they basically raised me.

I come from a working-class family. My parents would work for 12 hours a day, 7 days a week. Some days I wouldn't see them at all or maybe for just a brief second. Sometimes I would wake up while they were carrying me in or out of the car, but that was the only time I really got to see their faces, covered in dirt, blood, and sweat.

I wouldn't wake up because they would shake me or move me, but because I would feel their rough, cold skin rub against mine. Imagine that, five years old and not knowing what your parents' faces looked like or what their voices sounded like because you would only see them for a split second when you were sleepy in the dim light that the moon would cast upon their faces. But that all changed in 2009.

In 2009, my dad got in a work accident and fractured a disc in his spine. He couldn't walk, couldn't move, and was stuck in bed for about two years. I was only seven at the time, but I knew what was going on. He cried at night sometimes, asking what he had done to deserve everything he was going through. After the first year, he started going to therapy. It was hard for him to do any kind of physical activity at first, but slowly he started getting better. I was ten when he started moving more, and that is when he decided to put me to work.

I still remember my first day at work, the hot summer sun hitting the back of my neck. It hurt so bad that it made me cry. I wanted to work even faster so I could just sit in the shade, because the rays of the sun were blinding me as I wiped the sweat off my face.

My dad told me something that day that still sticks with me. He said, "Si no quieres andar así, ponte a estudiar, ¿o qué? ¿Quieres andar fregado de la espalda como yo? No, mi hijo, tú tienes un futuro en esta vida." Meaning, if I don't want to end up like him, I should focus on school and my future. Those words changed me.

Javier, 16 years old

I Am Tough

My family has helped me through some hard times in my life. For example, when I was in volleyball, two girls on my team made fun of me because I was on varsity, not JV like the other seventh graders. My mom and stepdad talked to the school; then a counselor at school talked to the girls, and the girls stopped making fun of me.

My brothers also help me. My little brother, Jesús, helps me by making me happy when I'm feeling down. My other little brother, Philip, plays with me when I'm down. My littlest brother Daniel says he will always be with me when I need him. My big brother, José, stands with me, and it feels good to have him by my side. That's how my family helps me when I am having a hard time in school and in life. We are really close.

At school, Ms. Blackmore has helped me when I need to talk about something deep inside. One personal thing that we talk about is that my first stepdad hurt me when I was small. We left our extended family behind and moved from Arizona to Washington in the third grade to get away from him. This is just a sample of the many difficult things that have happened to me.

My mom says I am tough like my grandma on my father's side. My mom told me that when my father was going to hit her, my grandma would stand up in front of him and say, "If you hit her, you will never be my son!" My mom says that I have the same soul as my grandma, the same strength as her.

I went through some very hard times when I was younger. It affected me physically and mentally. But now, thanks to my family, my teachers, and my own strength, I'm doing better.

Before, I couldn't talk to boys. I was afraid they would hurt me. But now I feel more comfortable, and I can talk to boys.

When students made fun of me when I was younger, I would let my emotions show, and they would bully me more. Now I have more courage, and I stand up to bullies. I also make better choices about who my friends are. I now have friends who help me up when I'm feeling down. I'm getting better every day, and I don't think about those hard times as much anymore.

Samantha, 13 years old

My Sister by My Side

When I was in the second grade, my life started to get complicated. I started to get bullied because I had trouble with reading, writing, math and speaking. I had to take speech class where they would help me get better.

Kids would laugh at me and say, "You're stupid because you can't do anything." When I started having friends, the other kids would scare them away. That made me feel weak, useless, and stupid because I couldn't defend myself.

Until one day my big sister Martha came from Guatemala to the United States. She noticed that I was going through a hard time. One day she came up to me and told me that I wasn't alone, and she started defending me from the kids. The kids started to get scared of her.

I was so happy to have her by my side—she made me feel strong, and she also told me not to care what the other kids said. She said, "Ignore them, they're stupid. Déjalos, están mensos, tienen cerebro de chocholito."

Victoria, 13 years old
Monologue from 2018 production of
The Hidden Truth: Unmasked

Dear Brothers

Dear brothers,

Both of you guys have been through a lot, but y'all still manage to take care of me and my baby brother. I love you guys even though I never, ever show it.

I just want you guys to know, whatever kind of shit we get put through, we will always stick together.

Yuridia, 12 years old

Yuridia at the top of Mount Erie, Skagit County, Washington

Mexican?

My great-great-grandparents on my mom's side immigrated here from Mexico. I do not know that much about them.

As a kid, my mom and her dad worked in the fields for a little while. Personally, I have never worked in the fields like a lot of my friends have.

I consider myself a Mexican-American, even though my light skin color does not show I am Mexican by blood.

Jeret, 12 years old

Madres

Cirila, mother of Eligrexi and Alfonso, with their grandmother, Julia
Photograph by Alfonso

Photograph by Alfonso

Photograph by Alfonso

"There is a hole in the world in the shape of you
Miss you like hell
I'll be wandering seeing you everywhere
Miss you like hell"
> *Miss* You *Like Hell* by Quiara Alegría Hudes
> and Erin McKeown

"Ya no estás con nosotros, ya estamos solos."
> "¿Dónde estás?" by Emanuel

Walls That Divide Us

Border wall between the United States and Mexico

The Wall

This is the wall.

When we say, "the wall," many of us think of the border wall. Yes, this is one of the many walls and barriers that separate us from our loved ones. Believe me, I get it. I live it.

Another wall we face in our lives is the barrier of communication that has caused many families to drift apart, including mine. And there are many other barriers like this we wish we could break down. We have been led by society to believe that there is nothing we can do about these walls but just accept the hurt and brokenness they cause us. But this is not true! **¡Ya no más!**

Our stories, we have kept them hidden away, until now. We are now sharing them with our community. And the barriers that have been in front of us, we **will** take them down with our voices. We will come out stronger and better than before. For once, we **will** be free.

Erik, 13 years old
Monologue from 2019 production of
The Hidden Truth: Breaking the Wall

Crossing the Border

My name is Erendida, and most of my life I have grown up without my mom. My mom is from Guatemala. She never talks about her personal life, which I get. I understand that it's hard for her to explain the troubles she's had. I know some things about her past, but I'm not going to talk about those things for my family's privacy and safety.

When I was one year old, my mom left me with my grandma and my dad. It wasn't because she didn't want me; it was because she was trying to keep me safe and keep herself safe, too. I wish I could explain more about that, but I just can't. We're still trying to keep ourselves safe.

When I was little, I already knew how to be independent. I remember enviously watching the other kids spend time with their mothers. As I grew, I would always ask myself, "Where is my mom? Why isn't she with me?" So, one time I decided to ask my grandma, and she told me the whole story about my parents. At the time, I didn't really care because I wasn't old enough to understand the things that my parents had done.

Soon after that, I heard my grandma talking to my mom on the phone, and I heard them saying that the best thing for me would be if I went to the United States. At the time I was six years old, and I still didn't care about it because I didn't understand what it meant.

When I was seven years old, my grandma started crying and told me I was moving to the United States to be with my mom. I was really scared because I didn't understand where they were sending me. We had to rush because in two weeks I was going to start my journey. The days passed, and I would see my grandma crying because at that time we only had each other. Finally, the big day arrived. My grandma woke me up and said, "It's time to go."

I felt really scared. I remember that everything went white. There were six adults that I would be traveling with to the United States, and I really felt uncomfortable because even though I knew two people, I didn't feel safe around them. They were gangsters who would sometimes come to see my family.

I remember that I was really tired. We spent like two days in a car, and then we finally got to Mexico. They put us in an old apartment. It was the ugliest apartment I had ever seen. It smelled really bad. They told us we couldn't leave the building or else we would get caught. We spent only one day in the apartment, and the next day we were up by two in the morning because we had to catch the bus.

I don't remember how much time we spent traveling to the border on the bus. After that we went into this big building, and they separated me from the others. My mom tells me now that they only had two options for getting me across the border into the US. The first choice was walking across the desert, but they knew that I wouldn't make it because it would be too hard for me. The other choice was to cross the border in a car, but that option cost a lot more.

My parents decided to have me cross the border by car. I remember that I got into this big, red truck and there were four or five kids in it, but the kids weren't sneaking across the border like me—I was the only one. The lady driver was really nice, and I spent two days in her house. After that I ended up in California.

I don't know how, but I just know I ended up in California. Then one of my uncles picked me up, and we drove to Mount Vernon, Washington.

When I saw my mom, I got really happy. Two months later, my dad arrived in Mount Vernon, which was great; but then I made a big mistake. I told my dad something I wasn't supposed to tell. My mom got really mad at me, and my time living with her was over. I went to live with my dad. Even now, I don't really spend that much time with my mom. I don't really care anymore if I get along with her. In the beginning, when it happened, I actually did care, and I felt it was all my fault. But as time passes, I realize that it wasn't really my fault because I was just a child, and I don't really care if she likes me or not, because I give up trying to get close to her and be nice to her when she doesn't try to just forget the past.

Life has taught me some really hard things. Even though my family members judge me, I don't really care what they say about me because I know who I am, and I know what I'm capable of. Sometimes they try to put me down, saying, "You're going to be just like your mom," or "You're not going to graduate because of what your family did, and that is going to chase you for the rest of your life."

But, like I said, I don't really care because I have some goals in my life. For example, I want to graduate from high school, go to college, and become an FBI agent. I know I can do whatever I put my mind to, and I don't need my family to keep on going.

Erendida, 14 years old

¿Dónde estás?

Ángel, ¿dónde estás?

I've been looking for you. I've been trying to tell you how my future's finally looking bright, how my worries and pain are finally behind me, how mom and dad are finally happy. Pero ¿dónde estás?

You always took care of us when mom and dad weren't home. You used to show us love and care. You used to take us to get coffee all the time, and we would laugh in the car whenever you tried to say the names of the drinks in Spanish: raybol, capchino, latay. When you saw I needed something, you would take care of it, no matter what it cost. ¿Dónde estás?

We need you. We need to be whole. We need you back. We can't be happy without you. Please leave the bottle. Please come talk to us. We will get through this. I used to hide everything, too, but it just made me worse on the inside. Ángel, please just call me and tell me what's wrong. ¿Dónde estás?

It's been lonely and gray without you. I just saw mom cry in front of me. I saw dad's teardrops fall down his face. I keep looking outside to see if you have come home like you used to every day. Isaac always asks where did you go, and all we say to him is that Ángel's busy. Please just talk to us so we don't have to keep lying to Isaac. He's just a baby. He doesn't deserve it. ¿Dónde estás?

I want to tell you so many things. I want to tell you that I finally did it. I'm finally going to graduate and become something many people did not expect from someone like me. I am finally going to go to college to become a teacher. You know, right? The things we always talked about when we were together. Pero ¿dónde estás?

Why didn't you come back? Why didn't you leave the bottle?

Mom came in my room and broke down and told me what happened. You were going to get deported. I tried to help you as much as I could, I swear, but it was too late. It was hard to find out that the only way to see you was through a screen on the computer. I wanted to grab you and tell you I love you and thank you for everything you did for me. That last time I saw you through the screen still haunts me. Ya no sé dónde estás.

All of the things I thought you would be there for are now just dreams. I thought you would be there for graduation. I thought you would be there when I leave home for college. But now they are only dreams. I just hope that you're happier in Mexico.

Ya no estás con nosotros, ya estamos solos.

Emanuel, 18 years old
Monologue from 2019 production of
The Hidden Truth: Breaking the Wall

Three Minutes

Is this the right place? I heard this is where la migra opens the border.

Dad? Is that you? It's Melanie. I am 11 years old now! ... Well, how would I know it's you? I haven't seen you in ten years! But they say I look like you.

They only give us three minutes. I know you live somewhere in Mexico, and when I visit Mexico, I feel that you are close. ... I don't know if the memories I have of you are real or fake. I do wish they were real. Maybe I have just seen pictures and made up stories by looking at them.

Mom and her family are always trying to push you away. I managed to keep one picture of you before mom stored the rest of them away. Every time I ask about you, they always change the subject. The one time you called me, mom didn't like it. I remember the last time I called you, you told me I have three stepbrothers. I wanted to ask if my grandpa and grandma were still alive. The reason I didn't ask was because I was scared of the answer.

I wonder if you'll be there for my quinceañera or other important events. I wonder how things would be right now if you were here. I want to hug you again. If you were here on the other side, I would hug you tight and cry in your arms.

I would also like to visit different places with you. I would like to spend four days with you meeting your side of my family. After we visited all those places, I'd want to know what you did during all these years we've been separated.

My biggest question is why did you leave? Did you have to? Did you get deported? How do you feel after all these years that have passed?

After all of these years, I feel sad because I feel like I have lost you. I also feel mad because mom doesn't really let me talk to you. But I won't give up hope of seeing you again.

Wait! What? It's been three minutes already?

I hope I see you again.

Melanie, 11 years old
Monologue from 2019 production of
The Hidden Truth: Breaking the Wall

Taken

You! You were wearing a black uniform. I woke up on a cold winter morning in 2013, and you were standing in my living room. You didn't knock or ask to come in. You just barged in through the door and pinned my dad to the floor.

You came into our home without any consent. My siblings and I stood there that cold morning, watching you pin my dad to the floor. I felt useless knowing I couldn't do anything. Later that day we were informed my dad was behind bars. For what? … Well, the "what" doesn't matter anymore, does it. Now my question is "How?"

How can you have the heart to separate families? He wasn't a criminal. He was a hardworking father with a wife, raising six children. What did he do wrong? My mother was left to raise six children on her own for three years. He missed our birthdays, and he missed my brother's graduation. One of the hardest days was Father's Day. We would come home with presents and wish to hug our daddy, but he was hundreds and hundreds of miles away. Locked up. … Why do you think you can take my family members away?

I promise you—when I grow up, I will become an immigration lawyer. Then **I** will be the one in the black suit. Helping families instead of tearing them apart. Guarding the door from people like you.

Noemi, 11 years old
Monologue from 2019 production of
The Hidden Truth: Breaking the Wall

Noemi (right) with her father and brothers

My Truth

I loved someone once, and he left me behind. My uncle lived with us for about four years but then had to leave and go back to Mexico, and I didn't really understand what was happening at the time. I was fairly little, but now I ask, "Why? Why did he have to go? Why so soon? Why couldn't he have stayed?"

Every day since that day, I wake up and miss him. I just want him to come back. The day that he left, I cried myself to sleep. Through it all, my parents told me he was going on a trip but would be back soon. I knew it was all a lie. Months went by but not one call from my uncle. Eventually I got really upset with him. I would think to myself, "Did he forget he still has a family in the United States who cares about him and misses him a lot? Does he not love us anymore? Is he happier in Mexico?"

Eventually my dad received a call from my uncle, and I got so excited and happy. When I got on the phone, I asked how he was doing. He said he was fine. I also asked why he hadn't called earlier. His response was that he had been trying to find a job but that it had been hard. His voice sounded the same, nothing really different, which I thought was a good sign. So, I joyfully asked, "When will you be coming back?" After that there was a pause, his voice changed to a more serious tone, and he said, "No por un tiempo, mija, pero cuidate."

Fast forward two to three years. My dad got news that my uncle had gotten shot in the left arm and lower back about six times and was severely hurt and in the hospital. That news hit my family hard. For a while my dad had to work longer night shifts trying to get enough money to send to his younger brother while still keeping his family on their feet. My mom was pregnant at the time and couldn't work much. A few months later my uncle was released from the hospital, and our family went back to how it was. No more nights and mornings without seeing my dad, but my uncle is still in Mexico.

My message to the government is just imagine if you were in my shoes. Someone I truly love had to leave me behind because of some "rules" I don't even understand, and I know he isn't safe, and most likely I won't see him for a very long time. **Just think about that!**

Maritza, 12 years old
Monologue from 2018 production of *The Hidden Truth: Unmasked*

Maritza, center, with friends

The American Dream

The American Dream promises happiness and no suffering in the United States. What a lie!

Many families can't even see their relatives. Parents have to work non-stop, and children work, too, to support their family. Children have to go to school wondering, "Is today the day I lose my parents? Is today the day that my parents will get deported?" This is a very real fear because children lose their parents due to deportation in the US every day. Imagine living like this. I don't have to imagine. I live like this every day.

Where is the happiness that is promised in that American Dream?

People believe that America is this place of happiness, but my family has not been fully happy in years. Whenever I talk to my parents about our family on the other side of the border, all I can see is pain in their eyes.

We still think about when my grandpa passed away, and we couldn't see him because of the border. We still think about when my brother was murdered, and we couldn't attend his funeral because of that same border. It still haunts us that the only way we can see our family is through pictures. It still haunts us that we will never be able to actually see them or touch them.

That's the reality. We are not living the American Dream.

My parents want to get away from the States. They want to go back. They want to see our family across the border before it's too late. But they can't. On the other side of the border is poverty and crime, the same crime that took my brother.

Imagine this—choosing happiness in Mexico but living in poverty and crime, or choosing sadness in the US but being able to maintain the family. Now here I am, living in a family that is trapped here, chasing a lie—the American Dream.

Emanuel, 17 years old
Monologue from 2018 production of *The Hidden Truth: Unmasked*

Emanuel on stage in 2019

If You Fall, You Get Up

In 2010 I lost my dad. He was deported. I was then only with my mom. I was the oldest, so I had to work hard in the fields and stay out of trouble. There were no breaks. It was all about work. I got mature really fast.

When I was little, school was the place where I could let it all out and be a real kid. Once my dad was gone, that all changed. I had to work hard. I had the biggest responsibilities—taking care of my sisters, working a field job, and helping my family with interpretation. I couldn't get in trouble at school if I wanted to get to college and get a good job.

I watch as my mom works so hard just to pay the rent. I always feel bad for her. I don't like living in this small apartment with expensive rent. We aren't the only ones. I see lots of people I know get stuff from the garbage. It's not easy.

My mom comes from El Jicaral, Oaxaca, in southern Mexico. I was born in California. My mom and I speak in Mixteco because that's the language my mom knows best. I speak Spanish pretty well, and my mom knows a little Spanish. I speak English, but my mom doesn't. I live with my mom, my uncle, and my three younger sisters, Rosalin, Rosalinda, and Rosalva. We live in a two-bedroom apartment. My dad used to live with us.

I wish my mother had never met that man—my father. Back in California, he had another woman, and my mom didn't like that. We tried to get away to Washington without him, but he came anyway. Then once we got here, he got deported. I feel like he ditched us. And I wish my mom had never met him.

When my mom goes to sleep crying, I always hug her and kiss her and make her promises. I tell her, "Someday I will have a house for you and a car."

I remember when I was little, my mom would always take me to the bus stop and take good care of me. Then when I was seven years old, my dad was deported. From that point on, I had to work in the fields in the summers. I had to work really hard so we could get more money. I hated it, so I would always try not to go. When my mom would wake me up at five in the morning, I would pretend I was asleep, but my mom knew me well. I would always have to go.

Growing up, I learned English quickly because I lived in a migrant camp and played outside with kids who spoke a lot of English. Reading has always been hard for me. I don't like reading because I speak three different languages, so I find it confusing. When I do math, I like the math, but not the reading part.

In the fourth grade, kids started bullying me at school. I was much more mature than the rest of the kids, so they rode me and made fun of me. I tried to ignore them, but it hurt.

After that, I almost lost my life smoking weed. I would always get mad at my mom and run away. Luckily, I had some people in my life that helped me change that. I am thankful for them.

I know it is difficult to grow up, but I have learned two things:
- If you fall you get up.
- You should ignore those people that try to stop you.

I'm so happy that I have people like Ms. Blackmore to support me. When I grow up, I want to have a job like she does, to let other kids know what's possible and to let them have a chance to do all of the cool things that I'm doing!

Juan, 14 years old

Juan, downtown Mount Vernon, Washington

Gone

Our names are Isaac and Jacob, and we are twins. We were born in Fairfield, California, in 2005. We moved to Washington when we were three years old. We're here to tell you about our life experience.

For as long as we can remember, we were both big troublemakers. We hung out with people who taught us the wrong path. For example, they dared us to shoot BB guns and break a window, so we did. We stopped being troublemakers because our parents kept getting mad—and for another reason.

From the time we were in kindergarten until the third grade, my dad was gone because he got deported. We felt sad and miserable. It all started when ICE came and knocked on our door. They were looking for my dad. My dad wasn't home. He was at work. When my dad heard, he went and turned himself in. He was sent to Mexico, and he was gone for almost four years. If my dad had been here during those four years, things would have been different. My dad was stricter. We wouldn't have been so sad, and we might not have become such troublemakers.

When he came back to us, we changed, and we started doing better stuff. When our dad is home with us, we feel better, so we do better.

Isaac and Jacob F., 12 years old

Not Your Perfect Mexican Daughter

Apa, ¿podemos hablar? … I have been meaning to talk to you because we hardly ever actually talk. You are always busy working or with my sisters. You never really have time for me. You never ask if I'm OK or if I'm upset. You just assume I'm "being lazy," and that's not true. I'm not doing OK, and you would know if you asked.

We used to have the closest bond when I was little. I would cry over you leaving me at four or five in the morning at daycare, I loved you so much. I still do—don't get me wrong. But it's just not the same anymore.

Dad, can I trust you? … You tell me I can, but trust is earned, and you haven't really earned my trust. You lied to me when you told me you would always be here for me. That hasn't really come true. Although you are here physically, and I really appreciate and thank you for that, you haven't been here emotionally.

I don't have the father figure I deserve, someone I can talk to without judgement. I wish I had your advice from a dad's perspective. It's always my brothers giving me the advice. They have been more of a dad then you ever have been.

Dad, can you just accept me for who I am? … Is this how you want me to be and act like? If I turn into someone I am not, would you be happy? Would you be proud of me for once? Will everything change, or will I just waste my time once again? If I let people walk all over me and not stand up for myself, would that make you happy? I know I talk back to adults and that isn't right, but I'm just expressing myself and who I am as a person.

Dad, if I worked harder and got better grades, would you be proud of me? … Would you be proud even if I got distant? Sometimes I don't work as hard because I don't have someone to help me at home. You have very little education to help me—you barely made it past the fourth grade.

Dad, if I dressed the way you want me to, would you be proud of me? … I dress the way I do because it's a way for me to express myself and who I am as a person and what my interests are in life and what I like to do. It's not because I'm a "tomboy" or anything like that. It's because I like to dress more comfortably.

Dad, if I let you choose my friends and the people I hang out with, would you be proud of me? … I choose the people I talk to because they help me through stuff. I can actually talk to them without being scared of a bad reaction or judgement coming toward me. They give me more advice and support then you ever have.

Yeah. OK. Sure. … I will always love you, and I will always know you tried your best. But has it really been enough?

I might not be the perfect Mexican daughter, but I do want you to be proud of who I am.

Maritza, 13 years old
Monologue from 2019 production of
The Hidden Truth: Breaking the Wall

Missing My Mom

People think of me as joyful and happy, but I'm not.

When I was a baby, my mom was sometimes around. We lived with my tía in Mount Vernon, but my mom wasn't really there. We lived there for a long time, but one day my mom and my tía got into a fight, and my mom left and left me with my tía.

When I turned five, I started to go to school. After school my mom would sometimes pick me up, and one time we went to get ice cream. The next day we went to one of my mom's friend's house, and we were making a sandwich when the cops came. They took my mom. One of the cops tried to take my hand to take me outside, but I yanked my hand away, trying to get to my mom. I was crying. He wouldn't let me go, but then I yanked it really hard and started to run to my mom. The other cop stopped me, and then my tía showed up. She told me that we were going to see my mom so that I would calm down. I stopped crying, but she had lied. We just went home. I didn't get to see my mom for three years.

In first grade, I went to two different elementary schools. In second grade, I stayed at one school for half of the year, then moved with my grandma to Kent. I stayed there for the rest of second grade. While I was there, my older sister moved in with us from her dad's house. She went to high school in Kent, but then something happened so she went back with her dad. I was downstairs crying.

I stayed in Kent until halfway through third grade. In third grade my mom got out, but she couldn't live with us. She could only visit for two days. Whenever she left, I wanted to go with my grandma to drop her off in Seattle somewhere, but I couldn't because I had to go to school. Every night I thought my mom would come back, but she didn't. I could never sleep.

When I turned nine, my mom came with my tía to pick me up. I didn't know it, but I was moving back to Mount Vernon. I just thought that I was going to be visiting for a couple days. I found out that I was moving when I asked how many pairs of clothes to bring, and she said all of them. I started crying in the truck when we left.

When we got to Mount Vernon, and we got to my other tía's house, all my cousins were there, and so was my grandpa, and so was my mom. So, I moved in.

It was crazy in that house. There were six kids and four adults. I started to go to school, and luckily, I still remembered some kids. My grandpa got a divorce, and ever since he cusses at us and drinks too much. He always has a six-pack of beer in his room. Now my mom has a night-time job. She goes to work at five in the evening and doesn't get home till three in the morning, so even though she's out of jail, I don't get to see her very much.

Anonymous, 11 years old

Sonoran Pronghorns

And then the animals, Don't you care if they come?
Because they come, too.
In diversity:
To cleanse the earth,
To feed our youth.
By putting up these defenses,
You become their nemesis.
Gaea cares, and she won't bear it.

Naturally, they'll cross the border,
Perhaps away from bombs to find water.
It's in their nature.
They shall mate too,
For the ingenuous genetic mixture.
Don't bring up your culture,
They don't see your rounded picture.

And then the phases, will you care when they come?
Because they come, too.
In extinction:
To change the earth,
To steal your youth,
To mend your truth.

 Rocio, 16 years old

Pronghorn doe with newborn fawns
Photograph by Helmut Buechner

"My writing comes not from the happy moments, but from struggle and grief."
   Isabel Allende

"They tried to bury us, but they didn't know we were seeds."
   Mexican proverb

"Every night when I would go to sleep, I would cry… and my little brother would ask me, 'Why are you crying?' and I would say, 'I'm ok, just go back to sleep.'"
   "Holding It Inside" by Estrella

El peso de las sombras

Isaac L. tells his story at Western Washington University with Joel in foreground
Photograph by Fernando Armenghol

Hola Mami

(English translation follows)

Hola mami,

Sabes me haces mucha falta, tenerte lejos es algo difícil porque hay veces en las que me siento sola y no estás aquí para darme un abrazo y decirme, "Todo estará bien, yo sé que tú puedes hija."

Mami, hay una distancia tan grande que nos separa y yo necesito tu apoyo para salir adelante. Es difícil no poder decirte que sigo en terapia para mi depresión y ansiedad y lo hago para no preocuparte, pero me haces tanta falta, mami, te extraño y te necesito a mi lado. Tú eres la única que me entiende y que a pesar de la distancia me tratas de ayudar.

Sé que he cometido errores y he tomado decisiones de las cuales no estoy orgullosa. Todo lo que he hecho es porque me sentía sola y pensé que de esa forma me sentiría mejor, pero no, al contrario, me hace sentir más mal. Lloro porque me siento sola.

Ahora todo lo que hago es para poder salir adelante y no fallarte y ser la hermana mayor que mis hermanos necesitan aquí. Pero mami, no quiero que te preocupes, todo saldrá bien y todo será como antes y estaremos juntas otra vez.

Litzy, 18 years old
Monologue from 2019 production of
The Hidden Truth: Breaking the Wall

Hello Mommy

(translated from Spanish)
Hello Mommy.

You know I really need you. Having you far away is difficult because there are times when I feel lonely, and you're not here to give me a hug and tell me, "Everything will be fine, I know you can do it, daughter."

Mommy, there is such a distance that separates us, and I need your support to succeed. It is difficult not to be able to tell you that I am still in therapy for my depression and anxiety, and I don't tell you so that you do not worry, but I really need you so much, mommy. I miss you and I need you by my side. You are the only one who understands me, and even though we're far apart, you try to help me.

I know I've made mistakes and I've made decisions that I'm not proud of. Everything I've done is because I felt lonely and I thought that was the way to feel better, but no, it made me feel even worse. I cry because I feel so lonely.

Now all I do is try to do well and not fail and be the older sister my siblings need here. But mommy, I do not want you to worry, everything will be fine, and everything will be as it was before, and we will be together again.

Just a Dream

Dad
I dreamed that I saw you again
In your brown shirt and your blue pants
You spoke to me when I saw you
I ran and hugged you with tears
You made me happy and took me places
You asked me, "Where do you wanna go?"
And I said, "Anywhere with you"
We went as a family, with grandma, mom, and everyone else
But then I woke up with tears
I woke up thinking it had been real, but it was a dream
A dream that showed me the happy times I had with you
I woke up forgetting that you weren't here
That you are still gone
I woke up.

Eloisa, 14 years old

Dear Joel

Dear Joel,

I just wanted to tell you that everyone misses you. You will always be in our hearts. I wish you were here so that you could give us advice like you would always do. I wish you were here so that you could make everything fun again, like the games we would always play. I wish you were here so that you could help out mom and make us all close the right way. I wish you were here so that you could take this huge pain away.

Esmeralda, 13 years old

Esmerelda's brother, Joel

Birthmark

A Rap

Life as a child should be nothing but fun,
Playing cops and robbers with the homies all day long.
Running and running away from the cops,
It's all fun and games until you get caught.
But little do we know cuz as kids we are told,
"Knowledge is the key to succeed when you grow."
And I never did, and didn't even give
Attention to any after everything they did.
Teased at school, even called me a fool,
I wanna end the pain so give me a tool.
Just wanna be the same, so tell me the way
To get rid of this, that's been on my face.

We all come from nothing and soon become something,
So trust the process, keep it real to 100.
We all come from nothing and soon become something,
So trust the process, keep it real to 100.
Heard many stories and reminisced the past
Moments are short, memories always last.
Thought about the future that I wanna be a part
But for now...I get to live with a birthmark!

Back in the past I would stand out in class,
Questioned "What is that?" is all they ever asked.
Defined by a mark, not by my character.
Is hearing out hate really what I deserve?
But why even talk? No one sees what I see.
Another kid trying to fit in society.
Getting talked down, I couldn't make a sound,
As I be getting clothing from the lost and found.

I was very different, but I was good at math,
Called everyone a "friend" but I was alone in class.
I can't change anything that happened to me,
Cuz hatred always lasts for all eternity.

We all come from nothing and soon become something,
So trust the process, keep it real to 100.
We all come from nothing and soon become something,
So trust the process, keep it real to 100.
Heard many stories and reminisced the past
Moments are short, memories always last.
Thought about the future that I wanna be apart
But for now. . . I get to live with a birthmark!

Daniel, 18 years old
Rap from 2019 production of
The Hidden Truth: Breaking the Wall

Stranger

I've been feeling like a stranger in my own house
Maybe I've just been in the wrong home
These doors keep me captive
These windows state my limits
Every mirror here tells me lies
Someday I'll knock down these doors
I'll break all these windows
And shatter every mirror I see
I know there is more to life than what my eyes can see
More than what my fingers can touch and feel
But there are chains tied to my feet
I can't escape from this reality no matter how much I try
I just can't
Not now at least.

Aracely R., 13 years old

Photograph by Aracely R.

Me?

All of you think I haven't been through struggles.
You don't know what I've been through.
The past is breaking me inside.
All these regrets are breaking me inside.

The quiet one in the class, all these kids,
Not knowing what I have been through,
All these burns, not a single scar,
The regrets that already broke me inside.
And when I say I am fine, I am really not fine.
I just want to burst out crying and cry myself to sleep.

Trying my hardest not to cry right now.
Not a straight-A student but not a failure,
Not knowing myself, not being myself,
No one knowing who I am,
Me wanting to die but knowing there is more in life.

So I keep telling myself to stay strong.
But I can't because I am by myself.
My parents not knowing who I am inside,
Trying to be the best, but they just don't notice.
Trying to be me, but that's when they push me away.
So I'm afraid to be myself around everyone.
I pretend to be someone, someone I really am not.
I wish people would accept me for who I really am.
So they can finally see the real me.

If they could accept me,
They would be real friends.
And they would love me for who I am

and not who I fake to be.

They would know how I feel

Just by a look, no words but expressions.

They would know when I lie.

They would know me more than I know myself.

We would have a bond no one could break.

Now they? They would be family.

Hilda, 12 years old
Spoken word poem from 2019 production of
The Hidden Truth: Breaking the Wall

Behind the Reflection

There's that one moment
I ask myself, "Why am I sad?"
I feel the tears slowly watering my eyes, but I wipe them away
I tell myself, "don't cry"
But the thoughts come, and I feel even worse
I let myself slowly drift to the mirror…towards my reflection
I see myself crying, deeply inside,
my heart wants to let it out…the pain that aches my soul
I see myself hurting
I keep praying, hoping something might change,
but you can't bring back the past
My head clears and I stare at myself
I see myself, not the reflection, but myself, faking the calmness,
faking my thoughts, and faking the truth…
the truth behind the reflection.

Eloisa, 14 years old

Holding It Inside

You think of me as happy and joyful, but really, I'm bad inside and out. I just pretend that I'm happy, so my friends don't ask me questions. I don't really tell anyone how I feel.

When I was little, my mom would leave my little brother and me with her friend because she and my dad were always working, every day. When I was about ten, I would take care of my little brother after school every day, but we didn't really stay home alone very long because we came home from school at four and my dad came home at five or six. My mom wouldn't come home until after nine.

Every night when I would go to sleep, I would cry because I didn't really get to spend time with her, just with my dad. I would always cry, and my little brother would ask me, "Why are you crying?" and I would say, "I'm ok, just go back to sleep."

Estrella, 12 years old

Hurting Inside

I remember the date—January 23, 2018. That date is forever burned in my mind. It may have seemed like any other day to you, but to me it was the day that I knew that I needed help, that I had hit my lowest point, that I was reaching my end. I didn't want to feel that way anymore, so I knew I needed to ask for help, or do something to end it.

I'm going to be honest, my only option to get help was to be admitted to Seattle Children's Psychiatry and Behavioral Medicine Unit, or PBMU, a hospital for teens who have reached their ending point. I hated it there and, like every other teenager in PBMU, my mind was obsessed with getting out. I wasn't thinking about getting better. I just wanted to get out.

And now I'm out. My mind is still on the blades that I used to use to hurt myself, to numb my pain. I know that it doesn't make sense, but if you look at it from my point of view, I was hurting inside, so why not hurt on the outside. I know that it still might not make sense, but that's how it works for me.

You see many people every day with smiles and laughs, but that's not always what's happening on the inside. We can hide the truth behind our masks.

Sometimes I feel alone, but, unfortunately, I'm not alone. There are nearly 1.2 million suicide attempts every year in the US. *

I've learned that there are a lot of kids who know how I feel. I've learned that always hiding the truth and filling the air with lies isn't the best way to keep going. If you want to get better, you can't do it alone. You need someone who can support you through your tough times. Don't isolate yourself. I know, because I did, and things were dark. If you want to get better, this is the most important lesson to learn. Don't isolate yourself. Don't shut out the people you care about, the people you trust.

If you feel like I feel, you probably feel really alone. I feel alone, too, but I look around and see that I'm not alone. You are not alone. Don't let the darkness hide the people you once had faith in. They are still there; you just need to find them.

Anonymous, 12 years old

* http://www.intheforefront.org/resources/suicide-data/

I Worry

I was born in Santa Maria, California. I have an older sister who grew up mostly in Mexico, and three younger siblings that I help take care of. My parents are very helpful. They help us think about our future. They tell us their stories about what they've been through because they don't want us to go through that. They want life to be easier for me.

My name is Aracely, and I worry.

I worry about my parents. They have really struggled to make enough money, both in Mexico and the USA. I remember being two years old and sitting in the bushes watching my parents work in the fields during the hot summers. But more often I would stay with a relative while they worked. My mom had to work nights and days. I didn't really see my parents often during my childhood. Usually, by the time they would come home from work, I would be asleep.

I remember one time we really struggled with money. My mom didn't have any work because she had just had my little sister. We could only pay part of the rent, the electricity was cut off, and my dad had to work double shifts day and night. I felt lonely at that time. I began working in the fields to help my parents when I was eight years old.

My mom is saying that I should start working in the summers a lot more, that I should go with her to the fields every day because we don't have enough money to pay the monthly bills. My older sister told my mom that she would quit school and go to work, but my mom said, "No." My sister misses school a lot—like, **a lot**. I try not to miss school.

106

I worry about immigration. Now that Trump is president, I'm kind of worried that my family members will get taken away, because then I wouldn't see them for a long time. I would probably live with my aunt and uncle.

Sometimes I think about going to Mexico with my family if they get deported, but it would be hard to find them because they say that immigration sends them back to where they were born, and my dad was born in a different place than my mom. My mom was born in San Jorge Rio Frijol, Oaxaca, and there's a lot of freedom there (in a bad way, like it's not very strict). It's kind of scary because lots of kids die from drinking and smoking. My dad was born somewhere in Baja California, but his family is originally from Oaxaca.

I worry about a close family member. She had a panic attack about two months ago. When we got to the hospital, they put her in a wheelchair, and they took a while to figure out what was going on. Finally, she was diagnosed with an anxiety disorder. They gave her anxiety medicine and sent her home.

I worry that I am losing my connection to my family in Mexico. When I was two years old, my mom received a call about my sick grandpa, so my dad sent me and my mom to Mexico. My dad had to stay in the US because he had to work and earn money to bring my mom and me back. My mom left me alone with my dad's parents for almost a month. Finally, she came back, and the news was bad. My grandpa had died. I never got to meet him or talk to him, which was pretty sad.

In the future I hope to graduate high school and go to college and become a veterinarian and make my parents proud, so I can help my parents, so I won't have to worry about them anymore.

I am still worried, but I am hopeful.

Aracely L., 12 years old
Monologue from 2018 production of
The Hidden Truth: Unmasked

What Is the Meaning of Life?

I always think to myself, "What is the meaning of life?" Is the meaning of life just gangbanging in the street, just fighting for control of a street, and killing your own people knowing that you might be killed too? Is the meaning of life having everything you want, but not working for it?

It took me a long time to find the meaning of my own life. The meaning of my life is being with the people I love and just working hard to have a better future.

A quote that I can relate to and other people can relate to is by Tupac: "Dying inside but outside looking fearless." That was me when I still did not know the meaning of my life. I was not proud of working in the fields. I was thinking to myself, "Why did God give me this life?" I would go to school looking really happy, but inside I was dying because I knew that when school was over, I was going back to the fields.

It took me a long time to notice that this life that I am living is the best life I can have. It has prepared me for the real world, and I'm always with my family. So, the meaning of life to me is being with the people you love and knowing that they will always be with you.

Anonymous, 16 years old

Anxious

Mom telling me about her country
what it would be like to live in her home
always telling me stories when I feel all alone
her stories always cheer me up
just picturing myself living in her hometown
my mom is from Santo Reyes Tepejillo
that is the name of my mom's birth grounds
it is a beautiful place that means a lot to my mom
her telling me stories about what it was like living in her town
how sometimes she struggled
how her dad would make her toys and beds
with his own bare hands
she is very grateful for her dad
she tells me he is a great and strong man
he has always wanted the best for her
he is very proud of his daughter and so am I
my mom is a very brave, lovable person just like her dad
every time she would talk about her dad
she would tell me how much he loves animals
just knowing that my abuelo and I have some things in common
makes me want to meet him now
I've always wanted to meet my grandparents from both sides
my parents are wonderful people that crossed the border
I thank God for that
they did it so their kids can have a better education.
Knowing that our new president wants to deport Mexicans
is making me anxious
I'm always scared that something bad might happen
while we're gone

I have school, my other sister, too
my older sister works so nobody is home
hoping and praying that my parents don't get deported
while they are working
I want them to see me graduate
to be very proud of what they created
they have created three girls that love them
and make sure they are appreciated,
which is why family comes first.
My mom and dad have taught me a couple of things
that are very important to them and to me
they taught me to be kind, honest, responsible, respectful, caring
and to always say please
I've been working on making them proud every single day.

Leslie, 11 years old

Agridulce

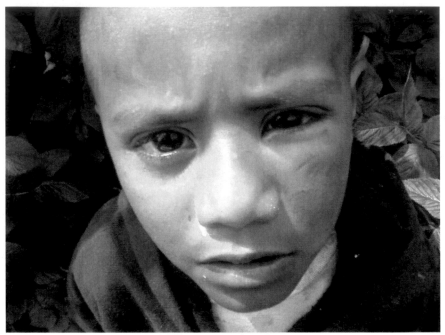

Alfonso stung by a bee
Photograph by Teresa Santos

"My mother ran into a snake in the blueberries. She was afraid to keep picking, so my stepdad killed it with a stick. Afterward my mom was paranoid, always thinking another snake was gonna pop out. A couple days later when I was picking, I ran into a much bigger snake. Then I was paranoid, too."

Photograph and caption by Azucena

"The rows—they will meet you
One by one,
But, the acres will defeat you"
        "Migrant Sun" by Ramón Mesa Ledesma

"Field work is hard, but we're getting money. We're the
champions, my family. We're the people who pack the
most boxes. I feel proud of our hard work."
        "We Are Champions" by Alfonso

"Sometimes when I'm picking berries in the fields, I
imagine building my parents a house in their hometown,
so they never have to worry about anything."
        "I Want Change" by Eligrexi

Los campos

Drawing by Ismael Angel Santana

Seasons of My Life

Summer

I start working in the fields picking strawberries in the month of June, raspberries in the month of July, and blueberries in the months of August, September, and almost October. It's my least favorite season of the year because I suffer a lot with my family. We get home with pain in our legs, our backs, and our hands. We get up at six in the morning to go work and get out of work at seven or sometimes eight in the evening. We don't have a lot of fun, but whenever we don't work, we try to go to the lake or the park with the whole family.

Fall

I am failing school because I don't have time to do homework because I am taking care of my little siblings while my parents are still working in the fields to get money to pay the rent for the house. By the time they get home, it is late. I am always so tired that I just want to sleep, and I forget to do homework. I try to wake up at four in the morning to do the homework, but once I wake up, my eyes, they just close, and I go back to sleep. Then I wake up at six in the morning to get myself ready for school. The bus arrives at 6:50 a.m. to pick me up.

Winter

I was born in winter, when my parents have to go all the way to Lynden to work pruning the raspberry plants and taking out the "trash," which means the plants that don't let the raspberry branches grow. They wake up at six in the morning and don't come back home until six in the evening. My little brother who is three years old stays with my oldest sister until I get home from school, and then I watch him. Once my brothers and sisters get here, they eat and help me clean the house before my parents get home.

Spring

My parents work in the tulips, helping organize the Tulip Festival, growing the tulips, then cutting them. My siblings and I can't go help my parents because you have to be more than 18 years old to work there. My parents sometimes come out at six in the evening, but they mostly come out even earlier at two in the afternoon. We have more family time because it's usually sunny every day, and my parents come out earlier than the other seasons. When we get family time, we go to the park, go shopping, play outside with the kids, or go to the lake. At the end of the Tulip Festival, we take a family picture with the tulips. It is a tradition we have done every year since we started living in Mount Vernon, and I love it.

Marcela, 12 years old

I Want Change

Every summer my mom and my siblings and I work in the fields picking strawberries, blackberries, blueberries and raspberries. When I am in the fields and I have some time alone, I talk to myself. I tell myself that that when I grow up, I don't want to work in the fields y mucho menos ver a mi mamá y mis hermanos working there. I want my momma and siblings completely out of poverty and not working in the fields.

I want a change to happen for my loved ones and for my community. When I see my mom working in the fields, my heart drops, and I tell myself, "I need to do well in school because, if not, this is going to be where I end up."

You might be wondering, "Where is her dad when the rest of the family is in the fields?" My dad milks cows, and he is always working. He doesn't come home until ten or eleven at night, and I hardly get to see him until his days off. My dad is one of the strongest and funniest guys I know. Sometimes when my dad gets home, he comes in singing and laughing. When my dad comes home in a good mood, he makes us laugh by telling us jokes about his cows. He tries to hide his pain, but we all know that my dad is always tired from working. And sometimes he comes home hurt from the cows kicking him.

Of all the things in my life, I am most grateful for my mom and dad. They are my motivation for doing well in school. My dad is always telling me to graduate so I will have a good job and won't have to work like they do. I also look up to my older brother, Marcos. He works every day to help my parents pay the bills— with a very big heart and a very strong personality.

Sometimes when I'm picking berries in the fields, I imagine building my parents a house in their hometown, so they never have to worry about anything. So their lives can be peaceful.

I don't just want change for my loved ones. I want change for my community, my people, people who are the same color as me. We all want change, especially in the deportation laws. It's not fair to separate people from their loved ones just because of some stupid law. One law can hurt a lot of people. It makes people afraid. It kills them on the inside and the outside. They have to go out hidden under layers of clothing. Some of them work from three in the morning until sunrise so they can disappear when the sun comes up. Some kids worry that their parents won't make it home.

Deportation laws make two types of people. One type gets money from the government and high pay. The other type crosses the border illegally for a better life—and then gets low pay for picking berries. You yourself end up eating those berries. That's why I want change. Gracias a todos. Juntos podemos cambiar nuestra comunidad.

Eligrexi, 13 years old
Monologue from 2019 production of
The Hidden Truth: Breaking the Wall

When the Dust Rises

If I could tell my parents one thing about how I feel, I would tell them that I am grateful for all they have done for my siblings and me. As a young kid, I noticed how my parents would migrate between California and Washington, but I never understood the reason behind it. Now that I am older, I have gained a better understanding of their migration. I've realized that they came into the United States seeking job opportunities and free education for my siblings and me. Like many immigrating families, they came in search of the American Dream.

I started working in the fields when I was 13 years old. This was a life changing experience for me because I was able to understand what my parents do for a living and how they suffer for my siblings and me. My parents thought it was a good idea to have me work in the fields so that I could learn to value school and pursue a career that kept me out of the fields.

I picked strawberries and blueberries. Picking strawberries was immensely difficult because it was painful to stay bent down picking the berries all day. While working in the fields, I learned to respect how hard my parents work for us, and because of their sacrifices, I will continue to work hard in high school, college, and beyond.

Sometimes when I go into the supermarket and see all the fresh produce, it takes me back to the summers I spent working in the fields. I remember the long hours bent down with my knees buried deep in the dirt. I remember the smell of sweet strawberries and the barn-red color that the strawberry juice would leave on my hands, with the tips of my fingers being stained an even darker shade. I remember pausing for a minute from picking, with my knees still in the dirt, and looking to my left and right, where I could see everyone bent down focusing only on the berries. Some were picking really fast, others were taking their time, but I imagined that everyone shared the same pain in their body from the labor.

It's hot in the fields, and the workers get exhausted from the heat, but they cannot stop because they have a family at home that they have to support. Near mealtime, you can often see workers begin to eat a few berries as they work toward the end of a row. When it is lunchtime, the dust from the ground rises as the workers make their way to their cars to eat the lunches they brought from home. These are the flashbacks I get when I walk through the supermarket.

During my junior year of high school, I discovered that I was undocumented and what that would mean for me. Prior to that, I had been unfamiliar with what "undocumented" meant, but I quickly realized that my path would not be easy. First, I realized that going to college would be difficult because I would have limited access to scholarships due to my citizenship status. Then I began to constantly worry that my mom and I might be deported, that we might be separated from my siblings, an idea that was devastating to me. Deportation would mean not only being separated from my family, but also that I would no longer have access to a good education.

Finally, I decided I didn't want to focus on what might go wrong anymore. I wanted to think about what I could do to make the best of my situation. I wanted to focus on my education in order to show my parents that they did the right thing in bringing me to the United States. I quickly began to build my confidence about attending college thanks to the support of my teachers and mentors. I want to go to college and pursue a career about which I'm passionate. Being the first one in my family to attend college is very exciting for me because I will be able to inspire my younger siblings to attend college, too.

Ana, 17 years old

Update: Ana is currently finishing her first year at Western Washington University.

A Good Job

I'm determined to graduate from high school and pursue studies to become an optometrist because I want to make my parents proud. In the future, I want to have a good job where I help people.

My parents have never had a good job that they enjoy. They have always worked in the fields where the weather is terrible, their bodies hurt, and the pay isn't worth it.

Every day when my dad comes home from work, hands stained from berry juice, shirt and boots dirty from the fields, he tells me and my older sister to study, so we don't end up like him and my mom, working in the fields in the super-hot summers and freezing cold winters.

If being an optometrist doesn't work out, I am going to start a small hair salon business, because I am very good at making hair styles. I get lots of compliments. I am most excited about where I am going to work, and all of the other unexpected things that are waiting for me.

I want to be somebody important. Sometimes I feel like we've never had someone important in my family, but my family is important to me. It's hard for me to explain why some people are "important" and others aren't. Sometimes I feel like my parents are "nobody," but to me they are everything, and I love them.

 Estefania, 11 years old

Mis sentidos

I see birds flying by
I hear leaves moving in the wind
I smell the nasty cow poop smell en el rancho
I taste sweet strawberries that I shouldn't be eating
I feel my cold hands in the morning

I see children playing and throwing berries
I hear the owner yelling at them, yelling at their parents

I hear corrido music coming from the workers' belts

I hear my family's voices around me:
"Get the boxes!"
"Give me another bucket!"
"Go leave the boxes!"
And the worst, "Let's stay a little bit longer…"

I want to be like the birds flying away

I feel pain
In my back from bending over the strawberries
In my legs from the espinas of the blackberries
In my feet from standing all day long
In my hands from picking, picking, picking

I see my dad's face turn red
I hear my dad grunt as he lifts the heavy boxes full of fruit

I hear children crying
I hear them saying, "I want to go home…"

I hear the truck horn, beep, beep, finally time to go
I feel happy because I can't handle any more pain

Marcela, 13 years old
Monologue from 2017 production of *The Hidden Truth: Untold Stories*

Marcela, left, with her mother in the fields

Family Divided

My name is Maritay. I am 17 years old, and I'm from Baja California, Mexico, but I was born in Red Bluff, California. I'm the second to last daughter in a family of eight siblings. I grew up in Mexico. I arrived back in the USA in 2016. Now I'm here in this country, the country of opportunities, and I'm a junior at Mount Vernon High School in Washington. I came to America to study because in my country they denied me that opportunity because I don't have Mexican nationality. I'm a citizen of the United States.

After I was born, my parents stayed in California for six months with me and my sister, whom they had brought with them from Mexico. The rest of my siblings were in Mexico, and my mother told me that living here without all of her children was not easy. Also, her relationship with my father was not very good, so they decided to return to Baja California six months after I was born.

Not all my life in Mexico was easy. The fact that I was born in the USA, and that my parents were away in the USA with me for several months, created a strong resentimiento de mis hermanos hacia mi. They were treated really badly by my tía when my parents were in the USA. She would hit them and punish them for no reason, and she would not give them enough food. When my parents would phone them, my tía would tell them everything was OK and would never let my brothers talk to them on the phone.

So, when I was growing up, my brothers took that resentimiento out on me. They would say to me, "Tú tienes la culpa de que papá y mamá nos dejaran. Deberías regresarte a tu país, porque aquí nadie te quiere. No sabemos qué haces aquí."

126

As I grew up, I understood more and more the comments they told me. They blamed me for my parents' leaving them when they were little. I was beginning to wonder if they really loved me, because they definitely did not show it. But time has passed, and now all my siblings are important to me, because they are always supporting me with my dreams here in the USA.

My parents have always worked to support us. My mom has worked in the fields in both countries. I remember that at home in Mexico, my mom was usually the only one there for us, because my dad came to work in the USA in what he calls "corridas," which means working in the fields but only for certain seasons. He would come home to Mexico during the off-seasons. In Mexico, my dad sold conos. He was a conero, someone who sells ice cream, popsicles, and all that kind of stuff.

My family's economic situation was affected by being such a large, growing family, because the expenses were always growing, too. For that reason, my parents decided to start their own business selling second-hand things. This decision caused us to see less and less of my dad. Whenever he returned from the USA, he would bring used clothes with him and then go to another state in Mexico to sell them for a few months.

When he would return home, he would immediately return to the USA to work in the fields—fields of pine trees, strawberries, olives, blueberries, and so on. And that's how it was during most of my childhood. My father was never there for our birthdays, holidays, graduations, or any special times, but my brothers and I understood why. We knew that even if he was not physically there, maybe mentally he was.

I cannot imagine how much my mother worried, and I know she worried because I could feel it. I always saw a worried look on her face. Imagine, my mother was alone with eight children. El dinero en casa siempre nos hizo falta, pero en mi casa nunca nos faltaron los frijoles para comer. My parents always made it work.

When I was 11 years old, I started working with my siblings in el negocio familiar, while my mother was still working in the strawberry fields. I did not understand why my mom still had to work in the fields when we had our own business. I thought, "Tenemos nuestro propio negocio, ¿por qué mi mamá sigue trabajando en el campo?" And then I started to understand why. There were days when we sold nothing. We have had our own business for 13 years, but my mom still works in the fields.

I moved to the United States to study when I was 15. Starting school here was a big challenge for me because the teachers spoke a different language that I couldn't fully understand. I was very confused as I tried to figure out how the school worked. It was complicated, and I felt very frustrated.

But with the passage of the months, everything started to go very well. I started to learn English, I made new friends, and I met many people who helped me. Now I'm really involved in school. I have had the opportunity to participate in the school's track and field team and the tennis team, and I have attended many different conferences and social events, including participating in concerts with my Mariachi class.

Last summer, I wanted to go see my family in Mexico. I missed my mom and my siblings a lot. But my dad did not have enough money to send me to see them. That was when I decided to work for the money. Not knowing much English, I had to go to work in the fields. I didn't do it alone, though. My cousin, Litzy, decided to do it, too.

When we told our family about what we wanted to do, they didn't believe we could do it. Ellos se rieron and said, "¡Ay! No creo que vayan a ir a trabajar, solo van a ir como dos días y no van a aguantar." Listening to their laughter and comments motivated me to really want to do it. I wanted to know what the people feel working in the fields. In Mexico, I only went three times to work in the fields, because my mom did not want that life for my siblings and me. She wanted us to focus only on our education.

I remember the first day of work perfectly, when my father took my cousin Litzy and me to the blackberry fields. I felt so strange. I thought to myself, "What am I doing here?" I never imagined I'd be working in the fields. Every day that I worked in the fields, I was very shocked, because I saw people who worked too hard. Despite the heat and the extremely hard work, they had a great motivation to keep working. I saw many classmates from school who were helping their parents to work in order to support their families. I felt tired. Honestly, I didn't want to do it, but I knew that I had to. No quería rendirme, sabía que podia.

Working in the fields impacted me in a big way because I finally understood how my parents had felt working in the fields for all those years. It also really motivated me to not let myself end up working in the fields all my life, like my parents, or like the parents of my friends. I want to be something else.

I want to graduate from high school, continue studying, and graduate from a university in anthropology or the medical field. I want to make my parents feel proud, to realize that the separations and division in our family have helped me to become the strong, independent person I am. My parents have tried so hard to give me an education, yo no quiero defraurdarlos.

Maritay, 17 years old

It Happened One Day

A Rap

It happened one day
Things changed
Ever since that day life hasn't been the same
I see the struggle now
I was just a kid
Didn't know what was going on
As I realized my father was gone
Took his life away by a gun
Wasn't the best father
Didn't treat my mother right
This happened in twenty-oh-eight
Years ago
Don't recognize his face
The memories are fading away
My mom decided to make her way here in the United States
That meant I was apart from her for months

While I was on the road,
Mom was struggling out there in the desert
Having to walk for miles, days, and nights
At night I was in a warm bed
While she was out there in the cold
Had the whole meal
While she had a piece of bread
I was praying for her
While she was thinking of us
Hoping we were okay

Momma had to find a job
Maybe two
To feed her kids, that was true
She struggled for the three of us

Summer days spent in the fields of the blueberries
I wasn't going to let my mom struggle by herself
So I took action and told her I can help

I was there
I wasn't the only kid
That was true
Hearing the music come from rows away
Heard cryin' babies up ahead
Hiding from the boss
He didn't want us there

Spending a day in a row wondering
When will we get to the end?
Picking up the boxes one by one
Cause I wasn't as strong
I was just a kid

I was watching the sun go away
Momma told me when the sun is behind that barn,
We'd go home
But as it got to be a habit
I stopped staring at the sun and got to work

Getting older
I am filling my own boxes,
One by one
Helping her with the bills, that felt right

Momma wants me to work hard in and out of the field,
Focus on my education.
When I graduate,
I will dedicate all my hard work to her
My professional career, hope that pays off
The suffering to stop at that point
The days in the fields to be no more
All the years of struggle
All the years of hard work
All the years full of hope

Azucena, 16 years old

Azucena, right, with her mother

My Mom Loves Me

My mom was sixteen, and she had just arrived in the United States. She was pregnant with my oldest brother, and she was living in Fresno, California. Shortly after he was born, my grandma died of blood cancer in Mexico. It was a really bad time for my mom. I don't know a lot about my brothers' dad, but from what I can remember from my brothers talking about him, he treated them pretty nicely. He had good money. He gave my mom money to return to Mexico to bury her mom. She was buried right next to the beach, a pretty nice place actually. I visited her grave last year. The rest of my older brothers were all born in California.

My brothers' dad eventually left them. He still lives in California. Sometimes he comes to Washington because there is work in the fields. My aunt always tells us when he's here. Sometimes my brothers talk to him on the phone, but they don't visit him because they don't know where he's working. One of my brothers looks exactly like his dad. One of my brothers doesn't like talking to his dad because he says he doesn't have anything to talk to him about. I don't really know why, but I don't like asking.

My whole family used to work in the fields. My five older brothers started going when they were barely five years old. They went to pick blueberries, blackberries, and strawberries. They woke up early in the morning, and they worked their asses off— six in the morning until four, ten hours every day with their dad and my mom. Then they started growing up, and everything they have right now is because they worked for it really hard. They have better jobs now, instead of working in the fields. Sometimes they go for a few days just to remember how it was. The jobs that my five brothers have right now are: building airplanes,

134

electrician, chef, military, fast-food worker. What I want to do when I grow up is be in the military like my older brother. He is like a role model. He loves me very much; he cares for me. He has taught me about stuff in life like working for what you have.

My mom met up with my dad in California, and they moved to Washington where I was born. We have lived in Mount Vernon ever since. I have worked in the fields off and on during the summers since the age of seven. It's hot, it's boring, and it's sometimes fun.

When I'm not working in the fields, I have a lot of responsibilities at home. My mom wakes me up right before she leaves for work. Then I eat the food that she cooked, then my baby sisters wake up, I get my sisters ready for the day, I feed them, and then I clean the house while they watch TV, so my mom doesn't have to clean when she gets back home. I have a dog named Rocky. My dog is not the best trained dog. He barks a lot and escapes sometimes. Every day I check on his food and water and take him outside to the bathroom.

My dad used to wake up, eat what my mom cooked, and watch videos on his phone all day. He literally didn't do anything around the house—sometimes he would, but just barely. Sometimes I wanted to go yell at him, "Get up, you have to do something. If you're going to be with us, you have to do something. Everybody in our family has to do something!" But I don't say anything because I don't want him yelling at me, and I don't want my parents getting into an argument.

My parents are separated. My mom still loves him even with everything he has done. He has tried to change, and he has improved. He comes to visit us sometimes, and he take us out to eat. Last time we went out to the theater to watch the movie *Sing*. And he's going to take us to Chuck E. Cheese for my sister's birthday because he wasn't here for her actual birthday because he was in Mexico. The feelings I feel for my dad are sometimes love, sometimes hatred. I feel love because he loves us and tries to do everything he can to change. He loves all of us. When I feel hatred is when he starts yelling at my mom or my sisters, but he wants to change.

My mom loves me with all her heart, and she wishes the best for me, not to grow up to be a failure in life. She wants me to have a good job, a family, and have a happy life. My mom is not in the best condition right now. She was very sick with breast cancer, but she fights because she doesn't like looking weak, because she's not. She's pulled through everything our family has been through. She stayed at the hospital when she was fighting her cancer. My sister-in-law took care of us. I felt happy and safe because she's really nice, but I was worried about my mom.

I visited her sometimes. She looked good, but I know she had pain inside of her, and she didn't want to show it. She wanted to be strong for us, mostly for my two little sisters. When she heard the news that she had beat the cancer, she felt really happy, and now she can go back to work in the fields. She only takes us out to eat when she's really happy, so when she got the news, one day she took us out to eat at a Mexican restaurant. I felt really happy and thankful.

After she went back to work in the fields, one day she was carrying the boxes of berries, and she fell down. She twisted her foot. She was also pregnant with my baby sister but thank God my sister was alright. But my mom isn't. I have to daily massage her foot and leg because there is a lump on her ankle that really hurts her a lot because of what happened. She's really stressed out and tired; she has to wake up in the morning, make food, pack it, get herself ready, and leave for work, all before we wake up.

Even though I don't tell her or show her that much, I really do love her with all my heart.

Elias L., 11 years old
Monologue from 2018 production of
The Hidden Truth: Unmasked

My Grandparents' Life

In the 1980s, my grandparents from my mom's side immigrated to the United States. Since day one, when they migrated to Fresno, California, they were looking for a better future, knowing they were leaving a child behind in Mexico in the hands of my great grandparents. They have been working in the fields ever since, from six in the morning to eight in the evening. They work all the time. Even if it's raining, sunny, stormy, or any weather, they still work.

My grandmother worked even when she was pregnant. My grandparents had six kids. Each of the kids was brought to the fields to work, too. If the kids were too small to work in the fields, they would stay inside the van, and every hour my grandmother would check on them. Her priority was to feed all her kids. Sometimes they would have to work out of town, and they would get up at two in the morning.

As the family was getting bigger, my grandparents began to notice that the money they were earning working in the fields wasn't enough to support the family. So, they decided to migrate here, to Mount Vernon, Washington, in 2002. They went right back to working the fields, but they didn't give up looking for better jobs to help support their kids.

Finally, they found one. They were offered an opportunity to work in Alaska, and they took it, knowing that this time they had to leave all their kids behind, not just one. In Alaska, they had to work sixteen hours or more every day with only four hours of sleep. Every six months, they would go home and spend three months visiting their kids. Eventually they realized their kids were getting older and they didn't need to work as much, so they came home. They now work eight hours a day.

My mother is the youngest child in her family. My mother started working in the fields at the age of nine. She didn't really like school. She wouldn't listen to her teachers. At one point, she ended up having a probation officer. She ran away from him once. She got pregnant at the age of 15 with me. I was born in 2005. My mother would take me to daycare so she could continue going to school, but she ended up dropping out and going to work in the fields for a couple of years. She now has a job that doesn't involve the fields.

Mayrah, 13 years old

Accomplishments

A Rap

I wear black every day
I don't bang
Don't wear blue or red
Just black
I want to graduate
I want to make my momma proud
I want to put a smile on her face
Something I don't see every day
I don't want to disappoint her with bad grades
That I don't get often
A's are the grades I have right now

Teachers telling me, "Good job, Azucena, way to go"
Checking up on my grades, hoping they didn't change
from a good grade to a bad one. Keeping it low key

Celebrating it to myself
Hoping it will stay like this for the next few years
Don't want changes
I want improvements
Don't want disappointments
Man, those are rough
I want to succeed
To be something greater then great
I want to buy my momma a house she has never had in her life
Don't want her to work in the fields
Man, that job is so tough
So rough what she's been through
If you have your parents that work in the fields,
don't disappoint them by getting those bad grades

Graduate, and then they won't be working in the fields
They won't feel the pain run through their backs
And they might have a headache, no breaks,
Not until lunch time
So they'll have to wait

So change that for them
Make them happy with them A's no F's
Maybe those F's make you cool but trust me they don't
Those Fs are proving that those stereotypes are true
Don't make that a true statement
Pay attention in class, don't slack
Don't get behind
Study for your next quiz to succeed
Don't fail no test
Don't doubt yourself
Ask for help if you don't get something
Ask questions during class
Don't talk, just listen
Take notes
Turn in things on time
So you can be something greater then great
To make your momma proud
So she can say it was worth it to come here in the United States
'Cause you did get an education that she didn't get

She might cry of happiness, then you will know
that you made her proud with your accomplishments
Way to dream big
You gotta put in all the effort to get on to the next level
To make life better.

At the end all of it is gonna be worth it
But only a few people have made it to that

Will you be a part of them too?
Would you be able to succeed too?
Will you be putting a smile on your momma's face?

Maybe, who knows, right
Just keep going straight, don't get distracted by all the negativity
Put your mind to your goal
Maybe then you will accomplish it all

Azucena, 16 years old
Rap from 2018 production of
The Hidden Truth: Unmasked

With My Bare Hands

Photograph by Nayeli

Photograph by Azucena

Photograph by Teresa Santos

"There is no greater agony than bearing an untold story inside of you."
    Maya Angelou

"Our stories, we have kept them hidden away, until now. We are now sharing them with our community. And the barriers that have been in front of us, we will take them down with our voices."
    "The Wall" by Erik

Speaking Out

Daniel performing at *The Hidden Truth*, 2019

Erik on stage in 2019

Dear America

Dear America,

I thought this was a free country. My parents thought they would be free and able to build a stable home. But no, they have had to hide in the shadows from immigration.

It is hard, but it helps me knowing that in the future I plan to help countries provide each person freedom, because we are all human. We have forgotten that this is a free country, that we have the ability to change and to choose.

Talking as a migrant student, I have gone through a lot. I know that I can't have what some people have, like a stable home. My parents don't want me to fail because they struggled to get here to give me a good education. I wish I could give my parents no worries and pay their bills when they get old. I want to make my parents proud not just by graduating from a university, but also by acting on the things I truly believe in.

Erik, 12 years old
Monologue from 2018 production of *The Hidden Truth: Unmasked*

"You can only accomplish what you believe you can." Moses, mi tío

Not a Free Country

My parents came to the United States thinking it was a free country, a place where we could earn more money. But I guess it's not like that.

My parents came to the United States thinking it would be best for them. My parents are from a small town called Santa Catarina Noltepec. It is located in southern Oaxaca. They lived there for 17 years. In 1989 they moved here thinking they would earn more money, but look at us, still the same, working our asses off during the summer.

Yes, I work in the fields, I am Mexican, and I am a migrant student. And you know what? I am proud about it. Working in the fields to me is one thing I am grateful for. Why? Because it makes me into a strong girl who wants to move forward in life, a girl who is motivated by not wanting to see her mom and dad working hard all day under the hot-ass sun just to put food on the table. Working in the fields also shows that I am not the lazy student teachers think I am. I know I am not lazy. I'm just tired from working so hard outside of school.

A donde quiera que voy o lo que hago, quiero que ahí estará mi mamá y mi papá, siempre conmigo, porque cada día trabajan por el mejor para mis hermanos y yo. Gracias por todo y un día vas a ver a tu hija llegar lejos.

(No matter where I go or what I do, I hope that my parents will always be with me, because every day they work so my siblings and I can have the best. Thank you for everything, and one day you will see your daughter go far.)

Eligrexi, 12 years old
Monologue from 2018 production of *The Hidden Truth: Unmasked*

Eligrexi with her brother in 2015
Photograph by Janice Blackmore

A Nightmare Come True

I scream and scream,
In my dreams,
In front of me,
Donald Trump looking at me

Remember the election, when they reported that Hillary Clinton had won the popular vote? I was **relieved**. I thought that my predictions were going to be right, and we were going to have our first woman president. But God had different plans for us. At around two in the morning, they announced the 45th president of the United States. It wasn't a woman. Donald Trump had won.

This is the nightmare that undocumented immigrants and DREAMers are living right now and can't seem to wake up from.

The day after the election, my friends and I had a long day ahead of us, reading our Snapchat stories, sharing how we were sad and surprised by the election. While I was scrolling through Snapchat, my thoughts were racing. Would my parents be deported? And if so, where would my four younger siblings and I go? If the worst happened, I didn't want to be separated from my brothers and sisters.

Then I had school. My friends and I were upset because we knew that things were going to change, most likely in a bad way, affecting immigrants of all races. And we were damn right about it. I know it's going to affect me and other people in my community. My friends and I might not finish high school because we might have to go to Mexico with our parents if they get deported, and the education in most states in Mexico isn't good. And it feels like the protests that happen don't make a difference.

If only Congress and President Donald Trump would make the right choices, that would be a way to make America great again, because we immigrants are depending on them.

I scream and scream,
In my dreams,
In front of me,
Donald Trump looking at me

Yaneyda, 14 years old
Monologue from 2018 production of *The Hidden Truth: Unmasked*

Dear Donald Trump

You don't know us. You think we're killers. You don't know what Mexicans go through in the fields—most white people don't like to get their hands that dirty.

I once saw you doing the Pledge of Allegiance. You didn't even put your hand over your heart.

You want to make America "great again." **We** make America great because we put food on your table.

You want to make us build a wall. That doesn't make sense. Why would we build a wall to keep ourselves out?

I was born in Mount Vernon, Washington. My mom was born in Shelby, Michigan. My dad was born in Madera, California. We belong on this side of the wall as much as you do.

If you walked into our classroom and looked into our faces, you might say you think we're "great." But what would you really be thinking? That we're all illegal? Useless?

You'd be wrong.

Tell us about **your** childhood. Did you work like we do?

I've worked in the fields since I was six years old, picking strawberries, raspberries, blueberries, lettuce. I hated it because my hands turned red.

Planting was even harder—planting strawberries bent over with my knees on the ground. The hot sun burns your back. The black plastic makes it even hotter.

Have you ever worked in the fields on a rainy day? When you get home, you're sticky and dirty and you can't even feel the wetness anymore.

What do **you** feel, Mr. Trump?

Student Collaboration
Underground Writing workshop, 2017

Rehearsal for *The Hidden Truth*, 2018

Dear Congress

Dear Congress,

You cannot take away DACA because you will kill our dreams.

It seems like you don't care that we risked so much to be here.

We came in order to pursue our dream, the American Dream.

Now you just want to take that away from us.

It feels like we shouldn't try anymore.

You keep saying that you want to help us, but that's a lie.

Why tear us apart?

Do you guys have no heart?

Esmerelda, 14 years old

Esmerelda at the National Migrant Education Conference,
Orlando, Florida, in 2017

Fight the Power

Benjamin, 13 years old

Justice for All

A Rap

Home isn't home
If you can't stay
Home isn't home
If it has to be this way

Don't want to see you go
Where would you be?
Would you be standing right
next to me?

The fence
The wall
Justice for all
Want to tear it down
Look around
Wishing it wasn't found

Separating families apart
Momma is gonna depart
Just gonna see her a few times
a year
Man can I just have her right
here?

I want to come home to my
mom
When I accomplish one of my
dreams
Showing her that I just
believed

Making her proud of me

I'd give my liberty to my mom
So she can stay here
For as long as she wants
Cause

She taught me well
To work for myself
Like she has been doing
Ever since she crossed that
wall

Part of me is saying don't go
But she misses her hometown
The place she knows about
But had to leave behind
because of
My needs
My future
And to establish a better
family

I know this isn't her country
Cause it doesn't compare to
her home

But it has many things
It comes with opportunities
Struggles and a lifestyle
It comes with pain
and a whole lot of blames
That it is our fault that this
country is going down the
drain
That's not true

It's
One nation
With the population
Immigrants full of education
Who are facing discrimination

Let them through
They want a better life too

They'll work day and day
In the sun and rain
They'll work day and day
And won't get much pay

To the flag
Of different countries
To the place I belong
And so should my mom

It's a lifestyle we've been livin'
Waiting for summer
Cause that's when we are
pickin'

It comes with struggles
And we know that
The vision to dream with all
these opportunities
That's what you are giving us

But
Change the rules
We are already living with
cruel
Pledge to myself
To spend more time with my
family
Cause in a couple of years it
won't be complete

You are leaving me behind
It has to be this way
You are going home
Why does it have to be this way?

The fence
The wall
Justice for all

Azucena, 17 years old
Rap from 2019 production of *The Hidden Truth: Breaking the Wall*

Azucena on stage in 2019

All Dead Chickens Go to Washington

My name is Rosalin. I live with my mom, two sisters, and my older brother in Burlington, Washington. My mom works in the fields picking berries. We have enough money because my older brother, who is 14, works in the fields with my mom.

When I think of Washington DC, I think of the White House. I would love to see it because the president lives there. Starting in January, we're going to have a really racist president, and I want to share my personal story to try to help the US understand people like me.

When I was really young, I thought that all dead chickens went to Washington DC because it's a big, big, big place, and I heard that when you die everything turns white. So, when I heard about the White House, I thought that the dead chickens' souls lived there. My first pet was a chicken, so that is why I love chickens so much.

I want to go to Washington DC because the farthest I've been from home is Bellingham, Washington, which is a half hour away from where I live.

Rosalin, 11 years old

Close-up for New Americans, Washington DC, 2018
Rosalin (right) earned this trip for her piece.
Pictured with Eloisa (left) and Marcela (center).

Scared

After the election, I did not know what to do. I am so close to reaching my professional dreams, so close to graduating from high school. I still have to start my college applications. This can't possibly be over. I cried in silence, not letting anyone know. I was, and am, scared of what is going to happen from now on. I just want to tell myself that everything is going to be okay, but I can't, knowing that I'm an undocumented student. I have come too far for this to be over.

My parents risked their lives crossing the border, leaving my three older sisters, my one-year-old brother, and me in Mexico. They saw a great opportunity for us. My dad came back and brought us to the United States with him. I was fortunate and crossed the desert the first time with my dad and one older sister. My dad went back to get my siblings, but they had to cross the desert four times. One of those times they almost died of hunger.

It took so long for my dad to cross with my siblings that it was hard for my mom to care for those of us here. She had to work and send money to my dad so he could try again to cross. My mom borrowed money from others, but they started to ask her to pay them back, knowing that my dad had not yet crossed the border. During this time, my mom had to find a way to give us food. Sometimes we went days without eating. My mom had trouble finding places for us to stay. After my dad arrived, we were able to finally move into a small house.

Ever since I was little, I have seen my parents working in the fields, watching them suffer day after day. I was about seven years old when my parents took all of us to work to help them pay the loans that they owed. The loans were the reason my older sister

164

had to give up her education in the seventh grade and work full time. I was little, so I couldn't help much. The thing I could do was taking care of my younger siblings. I remember crying in the fields when I was seven because I didn't know how to change my little sister's diaper. I was afraid that I would hurt her. Little by little, I learned how to change her and feed her. When I was about eleven, my parents would leave me at home with my younger siblings.

There are events that mark you forever and will never disappear in your mind. It was winter break, and I was just ten years old when I saw an ICE car parking in my neighborhood. I didn't know what was going on until I saw that one by one, they were arresting my uncles and friends. They treated them like animals. They grabbed them, tied their hands, and threw them on the ground, telling them not to move or make any sound. My dad was outside when they grabbed him too. I started crying, not knowing what to do. My dad was being taken away after all the work he had done to reunite us.

My dad begged the officers to not deport him. He had eight children to support, and he could not leave my mom with all the responsibility. One of the officers spoke Spanish and told him to prove it. My dad brought the officers to the house, and they saw my siblings and me broken into tears. He let my dad go and said, "Thanks to your children, you didn't get deported." We hugged my dad and were relieved, but everyone else was taken away.

I don't want this to happen again. The election results gave everyone a scare. My parents are scared; they do not know when ICE will grab them and deport them. I try to calm them, telling them that they have rights if ICE tries to deport them. I try my best to stay calm, but deep inside I am scared, too. But after all the things we had to go through, I cannot just give up and let the fear take over.

I do not know what is going to happen in the future, but I will keep on working my way towards my dream. I am not letting anyone take the only chance I have to bring peace to my parents' life. I want to be the first one to go to a university and give my parents a better life, a life where they don't have to work anymore. I have a dream, and I am giving all that I have. I still have hope, and until that hope no longer exists, I will do my best and won't give up.

My plan is to pay my college costs using scholarships, grants, and working. I will give all that I have, but if it ends up not happening, I will have the satisfaction of knowing that I did everything that I could do.

There is a Mexican proverb that says, "They tried to bury us, but they didn't know we were seeds." As long as my seed is still in the ground, I will keep rising up until I become who I am determined to be.

Rosa, 17 years old
Monologue from 2017 production of *The Hidden Truth: Untold Stories*

Update: Rosa is currently studying education at the University of Washington.

Hard Past, Better Future

Trump being president frustrates and scares me.

The Trump supporters want us Mexican immigrants out. They don't understand why we don't want to move back to Mexico. The main reason my family doesn't want to move back to Mexico is because they don't want to work their asses off for only a few pesos a day. Here, they still work their asses off, but they're paid more.

My parents came here for better jobs and futures for my brothers and me. If Trump deports my parents, I would go with them, and that would be difficult for me because I've never experienced life in Mexico.

When I grow up, I want to study business so I can make my own clothing line. A big inspiration for me is Virgil Abloh, the founder of Off-White, a popular clothing brand. I relate to him because, just like me, nobody believed in him.

I have had a hard past, but I know my future will be better. I'm just going to stay focused on my two dreams. I will have my clothing line sold in my own stores all over the United States, and I will help my family to finally get out of poverty.

Elias R., 12 years old
Monologue from 2018 production of
The Hidden Truth: Unmasked

Our Story

Society judges our covers without reading our stories
Assuming it knows who we are
Where we come from
What we've been through
It rips out the pages it doesn't like
Those pages written with the ink that runs through our veins
Those pages covered with the pain from our past
Those pages we don't dare to read out loud
Those pages nobody wants to turn
They don't bother to finish the book to fully understand us
One sentence
One paragraph
One page
That's all it takes for them to understand
To understand we aren't just the first chapter or the second
We are more than what people say we are
We will never be what they want us to be
We will always have our own culture
Our own traditions
Our own dreams
We won't let them change who we are
Because who we are is our treasure
A treasure hidden in our pages
We can be whatever we want
As long as we hold on to who we are
Most importantly
As long as we hold on to where we come from.

Aracely R., 13 years old

Photograph by Aracely R

Just Give a Thanks

You are asking me to thank you, but it's your job.
You don't come to me when I'm in the fields,
Thanking me for what I have done.
I get how it's respectful to just give a thanks.
But when I'm in the fields picking those berries,
It's like I don't get a thanks right in my face.

But I'm giving thanks to you for serving my food.
Giving thanks to you
because it's probably something you don't like to do.
Giving thanks because there is no one like you.
You are just doing your job.
Like no other can do.
So, thank you.

Azucena, 17 years old

Success Has No Color

In a beautiful yet cold world why aren't we better than this?
Why is it that we act like a person of color is new?
People don't have the right to judge me,
They don't know what I've been through,
And if they do, they don't feel my pain.
You know, I used to think I wouldn't make it. Why?
Because people doubt me.
But guess what? They are another motivation.
I won't be afraid to fail; success has no color.
I know that if I want to do something or be someone,
I will go out there and reach my goal.
Who knew I'd be standing on this stage?
My name is Anaelsin.
Thank you.

Anaelsin, 14 years old
Monologue from 2018 production of
The Hidden Truth: Unmasked

Fighting for My Future

I was born in Toluca, Mexico,
a small community just outside Mexico City.
My parents had three children:
my sister and my twin brother and me.
We did not have much money,
so we lived in a cardboard-like house.
My dad came here first to California.
Then he worked hard to get us here. He wanted the best for us.
Finally, we crossed the border.
My mom was scared.
We were separated from her,
my sister, my brother, and I.
My mom was by herself.
We kids went with a stranger who bought us
everything we wanted so we wouldn't cry.
My mom was scared, she was scared without us.
She did not know if we were safe.
Twelve years later we are still in the US, all together and safe and
happy. But there is one problem that threatens everything we
have. The problem now is "Donald Trump."
Now who is this "Donald Trump" you talk about?
What makes him so great
if he wants to kick Mexicans out of the USA?!
Why would he want to do this,
if we make up 17 percent of the population and growing?
We pick in the fields the whites don't want to pick in.
We pick for long days under the hot sun in the summer.
And now he wants to build a wall?
Where is he going to get the money? Is he paying for it?
Also, who is building the wall?

We are not building a wall to divide the nations.
Why would we build something
that is going to keep us out and divide the two nations?
We need to grow stronger together, not separate.
Donald Trump, why are you doing this?
I want a good future. Why are you taking this from a kid
who has a dream to be great?
We have to get up early in the morning
to go to work and help our family.
But you with your
"I started with a small loan of a million dollars ..."
The Mexicans that live here in the USA
just want a future for their kids.
They're not here to commit crimes.
They just want to be ...
They just want to be happy. I just want to make my family happy.
I'm here and I'm here to stay.
A young man with dreams from the little town of Mount Vernon,
the only home he knows.

Anonymous, 14 years old

Striving for Success

"It was 5:25 am. Very wet. The sun was rising. First, I saw my mom, then
the raspberries, and then, way in the back, the US flag. I stared at
my mom and thought, 'Life has been so difficult for you.'
It is because of her that I strive for success."

Photograph and caption by Azucena

Photograph by Valentina, courtesy of Teresa Santos

"We must dream our way."
    Pablo Neruda

"I reached for them
I took them in my hands
Those beautiful shiny stars"
        "Stars" by Aracely R.

"Now I carry my dreams in both my hands."
        "From Nightmares to Dreams" by Anaelsin

Cielos infinitos

Photograph by Aracely R.

Stars

As I looked up at the stars
Hope whispered in my ear
It told me I could touch them
But something inside me screamed
It said that if I dared to reach for them
I'd get burned
It told me that it wasn't possible
It said I should forget it

The thing is, I'm not very good at forgetting
So I didn't
I reached for them
I took them in my hands
Those beautiful shiny stars
They gave me hope
They brought me happiness again
I held on tight to them

I brought them home to my family
They told me to get rid of them
To let go of them
They didn't understand at all
They didn't understand those stars made me who I am
Without them I'd be nothing
I'd be lost in the dark

I held on to them
I keep them hidden deep inside me
I'm never letting go of them
They'll remain close to me
Shining through my darkest hours
Reminding me that hope still exists.

Aracely R., 13 years old

Photograph by Aracely R.

From Nightmares to Dreams

My dreams were once so distanced from me.
But the screams have silenced,
and now all I feel is peace.
I ceased my triggering memories,
The memory of a broken family,
The feeling of blood running across my arms,
and the darkness surrounding my soul.
In a place so green, how did I feel so unseen?
Looking back is never what I plan to do.
With hope that was given to me
I now feel peace.
With prayers
I have been released from my own shadow.
With opportunities
I know I am capable.
Now I carry my dreams in both my hands.
My name is Anaelsin.

Anaelsin, 15 years old
Spoken word poem from 2019 production of
The Hidden Truth: Breaking the Wall

Anaelsin on stage in 2019

The Dreamer

The dreamer is a beautiful human.
The dreamer has a dream.
The dream of no difference in America.
He is an undocumented human.
He works hard to reach his goals.
Does that make him illegal?
Does that make him different than everyone?
The dreamer doesn't think it does.
He sees everyone equally.

Anonymous, 16 years old

Dreaming Lights

A Rap

I'm living my life not living through lies.
I will live by what's already mine.
Mistakes are forgivable, all I'm gonna do
Is dream about lights that are up in the sky.
Life's a risk so risk it all, doing what I gotta do by the nightfall.
Everything is fine, all I'm gonna do
Is dream about lights that are up in the sky.

Visioning a dream, somewhere in the clouds.
If you wanna do something, then you gotta do it now.
Do what makes you happy, don't do it with a frown.
I do what is right without anyone around.
Express it, embrace it, you know the conclusion.
Think it, dream it, this ain't no illusion.
Have my head up high with my feelings down low.
There are obstacles everywhere, wherever I go.

I don't ask for much, but I'm proud to have a home.
Don't have second thoughts when you know I am gone.
I have more than one thing already on my mind,
Love, faith, and hope and thoughts about life.
Everything changes, nothing stays the same.
If you lived my life, you'd know all the pain
That I've gained and know all the ways
That I've done, just to maintain.

Don't you overthink every time you wanna bleed.
Believing in yourself is what you really need.
You're now a pretty rose that once was a seed.
Shape up your act, but don't overreact.

You only live once, and you gotta know that
There's no way back, it's just a simple fact.

I'm living my life not living through lies.
I will live by what's already mine.
Mistakes are forgivable, all I'm gonna do
Is dream about lights that are up in the sky.
Life's a risk so risk it all, doing what I gotta do by the nightfall.
Everything is fine, all I'm gonna do
Is dream about lights that are up in the sky.

They say I'll make it big, but I've never thought of this.
Some want me to lose whenever I'm gonna win.
I'm just like a bird, just flapping its wings,
Flying high in the sky and doesn't need to think.
Going and going and gonna keep on livin'
Faster and faster like I was on a mission.
Wouldn't even stop till I see a collision
Visualize everything when you listen to my music.

Don't be obnoxious, knowing I would accomplish.
You ain't that flawless, that's not an option.
They talk to me as if I was on the news.
But ignoring me as if I was amused.
I don't always show myself,
just like the sun and the moon,
But if you need my help, then I'll be there soon,
Cuz I wanna be real, not another fake dude.

I'm living my life not living through lies.
I will live by what's already mine.
Mistakes are forgivable, all I'm gonna do
Is dream about lights that are up in the sky.
Life's a risk so risk it all, doing what I gotta do by the nightfall.
Everything is fine, all I'm gonna do
Is dream about lights that are up in the sky.

This only the beginning, so why think of the ending.
Why give up when you could end up winning.
There's a war every day and we need to compete.
Look for a way, don't look at defeat.
Stress is a test that's gonna leave a mess.
I ain't progressed to be the best, this I confess.
Don't look at the bad while being on a cloud.
I am Lil C Boy, I say it loud and proud.

I'm living my life not living through lies.
I will live by what's already mine.
Mistakes are forgivable, all I'm gonna do
Is dream about lights that are up in the sky.
Life's a risk so risk it all, doing what I gotta do by the nightfall.
Everything is fine, all I'm gonna do
is dream about lights that are up in the sky.

Daniel, 18 years old
Rap from 2019 production of *The Hidden Truth: Breaking the Wall*

Tu felicidad

(English translation follows)
Me hace feliz pensar en que ya no sufrirás más,
que el dolor se habrá ido
y que los recuerdos ya no te lastimarán más.
No guardarás rencor por las cosas pasadas,
y ya no llorarás al pensar por las noches.
No sentirás dolor al respirar
ni miedo al hablar.
Podrás disfrutar del viento acariciando tu suave rostro,
a la lluvia cayendo del cielo lentamente,
borrando tus lágrimas.
Verás la belleza en los árboles
viendo sus ramas extendiéndose por el cielo azul
que al atardecer se vuelve de un hermoso color rosado
formando una gran obra maestra creado por un artista único.
Por fin podrás ser feliz
como lo fuiste a la edad de cinco años,
la edad en la que tu única preocupación era escoger el color de
tus dibujos,
o a la edad de ocho años cuando no podías escoger cómo vestir a
tu muñeca favorita.
Viviste tu corta infancia sin saber
lo que en realidad se escondía tras de un mundo
que ya no es como lo veías a través de esos ojitos de niña
ilusionada.

Sueños que duraron segundos
y la amargura que dura toda una vida.
Es injusto pensar que tu felicidad se la robaron sin siquiera
pensarlo.
Sin pensar en los recuerdos
que se quedarían grabados en tu memoria.
Pero yo sé que lo que ha pasado no es razón para quedarte en el
suelo.
Yo sé que te levantarás y cumplirás los sueños que tienes en
mente.
Porque a pesar del dolor que has pasado, los sueños no se
terminan ahora ni nunca.
Esta es una carta para ti, deseo que algún día puedas ser feliz de
verdad.

Aracely R., 14 years old

Your Happiness

(translated from Spanish)

The thought of you no longer suffering brings me joy,
To think that the pain will be gone
and that the memories will no longer hurt you.
You won't feel any regrets
in the decisions you've made in the past,
And your thoughts won't make you cry at night.
You will not feel pain when breathing
nor fear when speaking.
You'll enjoy the wind caressing your soft face,
and the rain slowly falling from the sky,
erasing your tears.
You will see the beauty in the trees
watching their branches spreading through the blue sky
that at sunset becomes a beautiful pink color
forming a great masterpiece created by a unique artist.
Finally, you will be happy
as you were at the age of five,
the age at which your only concern
was to choose the color of your drawings,
or at the age of eight,
when you could not choose how to dress your favorite doll.
You lived your short childhood without knowing
what was really hiding behind a world
that is not as you saw it
through those eyes of a disillusioned girl.

Dreams that lasted seconds
and the bitterness that lasts a lifetime.
It is unfair to think that your happiness was stolen
without even thinking about it,
without thinking about the memories
that would remain etched in your memory.
But I know that what has happened
is not a reason to stay on the ground.
I know that you will get up and fulfill the dreams
you have in mind.
Because even though you have had painful times,
dreams don't end now or ever.
This is a letter for you.
I hope that one day you can be truly happy.

Aracely R., 14 years old

Photograph by Aracely R.

Big Dreams

Thirteen years ago, my parents made the decision to move to the United States to give my siblings and me a better opportunity and way of living. In Mexico, where my family and I came from, they did not have educational opportunities, and going to school was not an option for everyone.

This transition was not easy for me because I did not know anyone in the area, and I did not speak the language. School was challenging for me because of it. I was placed in an English language learner program so I could learn English, but it took many years before I felt comfortable speaking, reading, and writing in English.

Once I was able to learn English, I decided to work very hard every day while in elementary school to help other students that didn't know English. I knew how hard it was to come to a new country and not know the language everyone was speaking. With the support of my family and teachers I was able to integrate into the community and started being active by joining a club, volunteering, and playing sports.

I am the oldest of my siblings and will be the first to graduate from high school and move on to a university. This community has given me so much that I want to further my education to become a teacher and give back to the community that I grew up in. I want to help those families that don't understand what they can do in the community or in their kids' school because they don't have much education.

Although I have the desire to further my education, many obstacles have made my school years very challenging. I am an undocumented student and currently have DACA, but at the moment I am on the edge of losing the opportunities that I have because I don't know what will happen with DACA in the future.

Another thing that has affected me recently are the addictions and domestic violence happening within my family. This situation has forced my family and me to move to different homes in the last year and not have a stable place to live. Not having my dad's support with me day to day is very hard. I will always be daddy's little girl, and I need my dad to be proud of the young woman I am becoming.

My family has always struggled with money. I have had to give up things, or limit the things I want, because my family can't always give them to me. I am not going to let these obstacles get in my way of becoming a teacher. Each day I am determined to learn and focus in school because I have a goal to reach and because I want to be a positive role model for my younger siblings.

My parents and my three younger siblings are extremely important to me. Daily I make sure that my family is safe and that my siblings are healthy. I help my youngest sister with her homework and make sure she's bathed and in bed for school. I am like a mother figure for my siblings because when my mom had to work late nights and early mornings, I was the one that helped my siblings with chores and fed them. Even if I didn't always finish what **I** had to do, I made sure that my siblings were happy and had everything they needed day to day.

Being the oldest child and female in my Mexican family is very difficult because my parents expect a lot more from me. They want me to become something great in this world. They have big dreams for me. I always try to meet their standards and make them proud. There are only a few of my extended family members that have graduated from high school, but they have not continued their education in college. I want to be the first person in my family to graduate from college and have a career.

Deysi, 18 years old

Update: Deysi is currently finishing her first year at Western Washington University, where she is studying to be a teacher.

That Girl

I've never been "that girl."
Okay.
That girl who comes out of a relationship and instantly
Finds herself in another,
You know, effortlessly, like it was destiny.
I guess it was just never destined for me to be …
That girl.

That girl,
Who never stops having people confess their unyielding love,
The one people can't stop talking about,
How pretty she is.
I guess it was never destined for me to be …
That girl.

That girl who knows how to flirt properly,
Who can put her makeup on flawlessly,
Who can post a photo on Instagram and not feel
A million insecurities lurking at the tips of her fingers
As she presses the share button.
I guess I was never destined to be …
That girl.

And I know that I shouldn't let this bother me, but it does.
It's like having a lack of male attention in this world
Is seen as abnormal,
As less than womanly,
And I'm always forced to ask myself, what's wrong with me?
But maybe it's because I was never destined to be …
That girl.

Maybe it's because I was destined to be something more,
To be that girl who just lives her life,
That girl who loves herself for who she is
And does not rely on male attention to make her feel all right,
That girl who knows what she wants and fights until it's hers,
That girl who still has insecurities
but at the end of the day just says,

"Whatever."

YEAH!

I want to be that girl!

Nelly, 15 years old
Monologue from 2019 production of
The Hidden Truth: Breaking the Wall

Obstacles of an Athlete

When I was smaller, I liked to jump around and run a lot. I know every child does this. I didn't do it because I was bored; I did it because I liked it. I love being physically active and aspired to do anything with sports. As you know, being in sports takes a lot of commitment because you attend meets and practices and come home late. I love it, but my parents don't. Considering they don't know much about the sports I do, I don't blame them. They were not able to live their lives to the fullest as kids.

I have done many sports over the years. This year, I joined a new sport, which was swimming. I did not know how to swim at all, but it's okay since I didn't completely drown.

In middle school I joined soccer, volleyball, and wrestling, but who knew I would continue to love wrestling to this day. In seventh grade, I decided to join wrestling because I wanted to try something that would challenge me, and because my brother had done wrestling in his middle and high school years. In the beginning, I didn't win. I lost and lost and lost. I lost every single match, and I got frustrated by not winning. I wanted to win. What made me more frustrated was when my parents said that wrestling was a sport for boys, and then my brother had told me just to give up since I hadn't won a match.

One day, I had finished my match of the day, obviously I had lost, and I was so bummed out that I had lost again because, for me, constantly losing isn't a great feeling. But then, on that same day, the coach from the school we practice with stood in front of me and looked at me and said, "Hey, keep your head up." I felt so happy and better because someone believed in me. Days went by during seventh-grade year, and we were getting closer to the end of the season, which ends with a big tournament. The last week of practice, I was unsure if I should even attend the tournament. Thoughts and feelings went through my mind: "Is it even worth it to go? I mean, I am going to lose anyway."

The day before the tournament, my coaches focused on me and decided to have me live wrestling * for about one hour straight. It was tiring, but I'm grateful they did that. Then the day of the tournament came. I had to wake up early and my stomach didn't feel well. I looked at myself in the mirror for ten minutes. "Should I go? Should I not go?" In the end, I went because being the person I am, I couldn't give up that quickly. At the tournament I was nervous and scared, and it was totally unexpected that I would place second overall, but I did. I cried because I was so happy that I had made it that far, because I had done my best, and also because I had wanted first place!

The next year I came back with more determination and placed second again, and I also made it onto the LaVenture Middle School Outstanding Wrestler plaque, which was very cool. I am proud to say that I am the first female wrestler to be on that plaque. I continued on with wrestling my freshman year, and I made it to the top six in sub-regionals and then on to regionals. This year, as a sophomore, I fought harder in regionals, and I made it as an alternate to the state championships. I'm pretty happy with my results, mainly because I'm only able to train during the short school season. Coming from a different background really makes a difference in my life, especially as an athlete. I want to improve, but sometimes there are obstacles that I cannot overcome as a fieldworker.

It is hard for me to be an athlete while also coming from a field working background, which as you know doesn't pay the best. In our family, we try to use money wisely since we know it's not easy to make. To get better in any sport you need to have good supplies, and more training if you want to be the best. But those both require money. I have been wearing the same wrestling shoes since seventh grade because they are so expensive. I cannot tell my parents to pay for new wrestling shoes and a wrestling academy because they will think I'm crazy.

I love wrestling and doing all kinds of sports. It is what keeps me going and what makes me happy.

Nayeli, 15 years old
Monologue from 2018 production of *The Hidden Truth: Unmasked*

* "Live wrestling" is wrestling as if you are actually in a match, so giving it all you've got!

Life

Not everyone has the same life.
Not everyone feels alive.
I live surviving on beans and rice.
But I don't despise the life I got.
Sure, it's crazy.
Never feelin' lazy.
Working hard, but always feelin' a lil crazy.
But don't worry, cuz in my mind it's all straight.
Always feelin' great.
Surely, I make mistakes.
But I never regret the things done.
Or the things that come off of my tongue.
Never a slump.
Things do get hard.
You don't have to cry.
It's all going to be all right.
Life won't fix itself overnight.
But don't worry, we won't stop fighting tonight.

José, 17 years old

Flowers, People, No Difference

Flowers, beautiful, aren't they?

Colores hermosos, pétalos y olores distintos,

People, beautiful and unique in their own ways,

Smart, athletic and able to communicate.

同じではない花と人々は何も違いはありません。

Flowers come and go,

But you never forget how they look and smell.

Personas cambian,

But are never forgotten for their unique ways of living.

똑같지 마십시오. 꽃과 사람들은 전혀 다릅니다.

Common flowers in different colors,

Extraño pero no diferente.

People with different languages, like:

Spanish Hola,

Korean 안녕하세요,

Japanese こんにちは,

And Greek Χαίρετε,

But not different from the rest.

Μην είστε οι ίδιοι Λουλούδια και οι άνθρωποι δεν είναι τίποτα διαφορετικό.

Everyone is different.

There is no one the same as you.

You're unique and different from the rest.

なぜ同じである?

When you can be yourself,

and be known differently from the rest!

Just like flowers are different for how they look and smell.

Be known for your unique style and differences.

똑같지 마라!!!

It seems like someone just made a copy of another person,

But even if a flower were to be the same,

Todas tienen algo diferente.
People are different but just don't show it,
They cover it up,
By looking the same as the rest.
It's as if they were,
부, ペースト, επαναλαμβάνω.
Every day, all the time,
If you follow the trend, it's cool.
If you don't follow the trend, it's cool.
Por enseñando quien eres, tú eres bueno.
Being unique in this world is wonderful because
Flowers and people share that same uniqueness.

Nelly, 14 years old

Drawing by Francisco Cruz

Greater Dreams

Growing up, education wasn't very important to my parents. All they wanted was for my siblings and me to attend school and graduate. Nothing more. They themselves did not get a good education. They both had to drop out at a young age to help their families work and make a living. They thought that once we finished high school, we would start working right away.

None of my siblings really enjoyed school, and they were basically going just to follow what my parents had told us to do. For me, I've loved school since my first day of preschool. I loved learning about new subjects and everything, but when I would go home to share with my parents what I learned that day, they would just say "great" and go back to what they were doing.

I never got the support I wanted from them to try my best in school. Even when I did extra-curricular activities, or when I would bring home report cards with straight A's, they didn't seem to be any happier or prouder than if I hadn't. The same thing happened with my older siblings; they got no response from my parents, but it worked out for them because they didn't want or need that extra push. I, however, would have liked it.

I remember when I was younger, I never understood why they weren't encouraging me to try my best in school until I got older. I realized the reason they never put in any effort was because they didn't know how to. I don't blame my parents for any of this whatsoever, because they honestly didn't know anything about school. All they knew was work.

Because of their lack of reaction to anything school-related, I began to think that maybe I would just finish high school and somehow find a job that required no further education. For the longest time, I genuinely thought I was not going to college. Then I started thinking, am I really going to limit myself from accomplishing greater things?

I finally concluded that I'm not stopping at high school. I will get a masters in a major I'm passionate about. I'm still not going to stop after that. I will continue to learn more with or without the support of others. For my parents, my high school diploma will be enough, but it is not for me.

Griselda, 16 years old

"A book, too, can be a star, a living fire to lighten the darkness, leading out into the expanding universe."
Madeleine L'Engle

"Each of us is born with a box of matches inside us but we can't strike them all by ourselves."
Like Water for Chocolate by Laura Esquivel

"My goal is to create spaces where people will listen, so the students feel heard, and oppressive systems begin to break down."
"Reflections from an Educator" by Janice Blackmore

Afterword

MOUNT VERNON

MIGRANT LEADERS CLUB

Mount Vernon Migrant Leaders Club

The Migrant Leaders Club was created ten years ago to support migrant students' efforts to complete high school. Migrant students come from families who migrate to find work in agriculture, fishing, and logging. These students struggle to graduate for many reasons: educational interruptions from frequent family moves, cultural and language barriers, trauma from a broken immigration system, an educational system that fails to value their strengths, and poverty that requires them to work alongside their parents.

Rooted in the belief that migrant students need a safe space from which they can explore the healing work of personal storytelling, the club cultivates youth voice and leadership in a student-driven environment where responsibility and expectations increase over time. Today the club serves approximately 75 students annually in the Mount Vernon School District (MVSD), through weekly meetings at the high school and two middle schools.

Migrant students often feel marginalized among their classmates and find solace in connecting with students who share similar life experiences. Many live in extreme poverty, with families of eight surviving on less than $25,000 per year. Children often begin summer work in the fields while still in elementary school—this is typically when the ridicule and shame begin.

The Migrant Leaders Club works to turn that shame into pride. Through personal storytelling, peer support, traveling, and public speaking, students gain opportunities to see themselves, and be seen by others, as emerging leaders Although the club began with an emphasis on high school graduation, club members have developed their own goals over the years: first, to educate others about being migrant while also educating themselves; and second, to embrace and showcase their own unique talents.

With these goals in mind, the club has focused on several ambitious projects over the years. Their first anthology of student writing, *DreamFields: A Peek into the World of Migrant Youth,* was published in 2012 and has sold more than 1,600 copies. In 2015, the club inspired and starred in an award-winning documentary titled *Every Row a Path*, created by filmmaker Jill Freidberg in partnership with Reel Grrls. For the past four years, the club has also been collaborating with partner organization Underground Writing on creative writing workshops and content for this anthology and other projects. The proceeds from all these endeavors fund travel and college scholarships for local migrant students, with more than $13,000 in scholarship money raised so far.

Migrant Leaders Club founder and adviser, Janice Blackmore, has a passion for supporting local farmworker families, especially those from indigenous areas of southern Mexico, where she lived at one time. Her desire to disrupt the cycles of poverty for migrant farmworkers began in her teens when she formed enduring friendships with migrant farmworker families in Eastern Washington.

Mount Vernon Migrant Leaders Club

For information regarding programs, speaking and consulting, volunteering, or donations, please contact us:

e | migrantleadersclub@gmail.com
w | www.migrantleadersclub.org

DreamFields: A Peek into the World of Migrant Youth is available at www.amazon.com.
The documentary *Every Row a Path* is available at www.everyrow.com.

Mount Vernon Migrant Leaders Club, Mount Vernon High School
Club advisor Janice Blackmore far right in the second row

Local Migrant Student Facts

- Graduation rate for migrant students in Washington State: **68%**
- MVSD students who receive free or reduced lunch: **62%**
- MVSD Latino population: **55%**
- MVSD migrant population: **13%**
- MVSD migrant students' ethnic origins: **98%** Mexican; **80%** indigenous Mexican
- Common languages spoken by MVSD migrant students: **English, Spanish, Mixteco, Triqui**
- Age migrant students typically begin summer field work: **6–13 years old**

Underground Writing

During a creative writing workshop with the Migrant Leaders Club—a quiet time of revision and editing—a notebook was passed down the row of students and placed in front of me for feedback. On the page I saw the name of a student who we'd been hoping would eventually tell her story. I leaned forward slightly and looked down the row. The student was leaning over a piece of paper, writing—or acting like she was. I didn't press the point. What had been passed down the row was what needed to be communicated. It was beautifully written, and sad. It seemed almost to radiate on the page, as if each word were a match, each sentence a piece of tinder.

There have been countless moments like this in the four years we've been working with the Migrant Leaders Club. What has grown into a generative collaboration began when we first met Janice Blackmore, founder and advisor for the club, in June 2015. Underground Writing was a few weeks out from its official launch, and we were meeting with Janice to talk about the Migrant Leaders Club becoming our second site. Given the fact that one of the primary goals of the club is having the students tell their stories, the idea of facilitated writing times interested her immediately. The dialogue continued over a number of months, and in early October 2015 we officially launched our site with the club.

The first couple of workshops we facilitated in the fall of 2015 were full of brainstorming—ideas, ice breakers, nervous laughter. In our aim to present writing as an art form and a tool for life, we were up for whatever best served the students.
And then there was silence. Lots of it. It wasn't necessarily uncomfortable, but the site was new, and we couldn't tell if the

students were connecting with the literature and writing in the way we had hoped. Slowly but surely, however, the writing began to add up through both typical and unusual workshop formats. The students led. We followed with paper and pencils. And the writings kept getting passed down the row for us to provide feedback on, edit, and experience. All of them—no matter the subject—were luminous.

It has been a beautiful collaboration from the start. Writings that grew out of the workshops have been presented at conferences and colleges, appeared in newsletters, and have been published in books. They have been performed annually on stage in *The Hidden Truth* at the historic Lincoln Theatre in Mount Vernon. Some of the personal narratives were even shared onstage at The Public Theater in New York City—15 students were given the featured audience talkback spotlight following a performance of *Miss You Like Hell*, a musical by Quiara Alegría Hudes.

The students in the Migrant Leaders Club have grown as writers. There is now, broadly speaking, a culture of writing within the club. They've learned to make choices of revision. They've learned to push back on editing recommendations. And I'd suggest that the students have become, through the process of writing, more aware of both themselves and the world around them. Whether they know it or not, they have challenged me to confront suffering and eradicate indifference. They have allowed me to learn more about racism and its continuing impact. They've invited me to see the brokenness they hold within. And my own as well.

Last week, doing research for an essay, I rediscovered the myth of Prometheus. Though forbidden by the gods to introduce fire to humanity, Prometheus vows: "Mankind shall have fire in spite

of the tyrant who sits on the mountain top." The myth seems
current, and can work in a variety of metaphoric ways, but I see
this mythological fire as language. The written word. The stories
and poetry and raps of the Migrant Leaders Club that will be
written no matter who is in power, who is elite, or who is
listening. Through working with these students, I am different. I
have stood in the flames and been transformed.

Matt Malyon
Founder, Director, and Teaching Writer | Underground Writing
www.undergroundwriting.org

Underground Writing is a literature-based creative writing program serving migrant, incarcerated, recovery, and other at-risk communities in northern Washington through literacy and personal transformation. We facilitate generative readings of literature spanning the tradition—from ancient texts to those written in our workshops. Honoring the transforming power of the word, we believe that attentive reading leads to attentive writing, and that attentive writing has the power to assist in the restoration of communities, the imagination, and individual lives.

For information regarding programs, speaking and consulting, volunteering, or donations, please contact us.

Underground Writing
P.O. Box 1043
Mount Vernon, WA 98273

360.220.0467
e | info@undergroundwriting.org
w | www.undergroundwriting.org

Workshop Sites
Mount Vernon Migrant Leaders Club
Skagit County Community Justice Center
Skagit County Juvenile Detention
Skagit Valley Recovery Community
YMCA Oasis Daylight Center

Tearing Down Walls

In the spring of 2018, members of the Mount Vernon Migrant Leaders Club accepted an invitation to travel to New York City to see a musical at The Public Theatre. The play, *Miss You Like Hell* by Quiara Alegría Hudes and Erin McKeown, explores the damage and heartbreak that US immigration policy has inflicted on immigrant families. Inspired by their New York City experience, the students decided to turn their annual spring showcase, *The Hidden Truth: Breaking the Wall,* into a theatrical event.

Underground Writing had been collaborating with the Migrant Leaders Club since 2015. In addition to leading regular writing workshops, we had helped with previous productions of *The Hidden Truth.* This year, though, we committed our workshops to exploring a new genre and developing dramatic pieces for the upcoming show.

Throughout the fall of 2018, students wrote and rewrote monologues, short scenes, poetry, and rap lyrics. Rehearsals began after winter break, and we worked together to shift the writing from notebook to stage. As opening night approached, students who did not write material for the show stepped into the roles of student director, stage manager, graphic artist, and camera crew.

In one lively rehearsal discussion, someone mentioned the fall of the Berlin Wall, an event that occurred well before these high school and middle school students were born. The image of a wall coming down, the group decided, was more powerful than the image of a wall going up.

This idea took shape in the scene shop (Barry Hendrix's woodworking studio) as a replica of a section of the fence on the southern border between the United States and Mexico. Stark and slatted, 10 feet long and 7 feet tall, the fence rolled on stage at the start of the show. The lights cast the shadow of slats onto the desert backdrop, which loomed over every monologue, every poem, and every rap.

The fence became a rolling metaphor for the many barriers, both literal and figurative, that migrant students face. The threat of deportation. Broken families. Depression and anxiety. Too little money for too much work. Low expectations and unfair assumptions at school.

At the climax of the show, however, the fence was transformed into a symbol of overcoming as the performers dismantled it, line by line and slat by slat. In the words of Erik, a middle school student, "The barriers that have been in front of us, we will take them down with our voices."

And they did.

Now that the curtain has come down on *The Hidden Truth: Breaking the Wall*, these voices will continue to resonate in the hearts and minds of their audience through the pages of *When the Dust Rises*. Here's to more walls coming down—and more curtains going up.

Jennifer Morison Hendrix
Playwright
Teaching Writer and Editor | Underground Writing
www.morisonhendrix.com

The Hidden Truth in Pictures

With the cast and crew of *Miss You Like Hell*,
The Public Theatre, New York City, 2018

Rehearsal for *The Hidden Truth,* 2019
Photograph by Jennifer Morison Hendrix

Set on opening night

Tearing down the wall

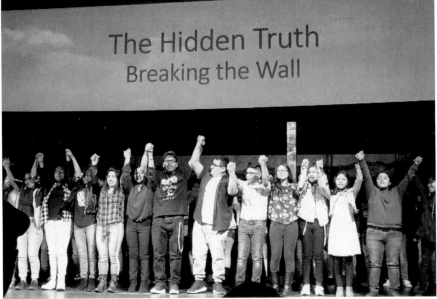

Curtain call

Traveling Farther Afield

The high point of the Migrant Leaders Club experience is the chance to travel, often beyond the state of Washington, to speak publicly at conferences, schools, and events. Club members have traveled throughout the United States to share their stories at conferences, colleges and universities, and with other migrant youth leaders.

National Migrant Education Conference, Orlando, Florida, 2013

Kentucky, 2013

National Migrant Education Conference, San Antonio, Texas, 2014

En route to Murray State University, Kentucky, 2014

Oaxaqueño Youth Encuentro, California, 2015

New York City, 2015

National Migrant Education Conference, Seattle, Washington, 2015

Oaxaqueño Youth Encuentro, California, 2016

National Migrant Education Conference, San Diego, California, 2016

National Migrant Education Conference, Orlando, Florida, 2017

Oaxaqueño Youth Encuentro, California, 2017

Liberty Island, New York City, 2018

National Migrant Education Conference, Portland, Oregon, 2018

Washington State Migrant Conference, Yakima, Washington, 2018

Oaxaqueño Youth Encuentro, California, 2018

Dartmouth College, Hanover, New Hampshire, 2019

Reflections from an Educator

"An educator in a system of oppression is either a revolutionary or an oppressor." — Lerone Bennett, Jr.

As the adviser for the Migrant Leaders Club, I have been asked many times over the years, "How do you do it? What is your formula? How do I replicate the work you are doing with your students?" I used to shy away from these questions because to answer them fully, I would have needed to delve deeply into uncomfortable conversations about how our country is failing our youth—and our individual roles in that failure.

However, my students have helped me to see that we must have these uncomfortable conversations. They have shown me that there is an urgency to this work I do, as unsettling as it may be.

Oppression and Privilege

As a school district employee tasked with supporting migrant students, my work feels maddening at times. This is because I work from within the historically oppressive US education system, a system designed not for migrant student success, but rather, some would argue, for their failure. A system built on the belief that students in certain racial and socioeconomic groups are superior to others. A system that consistently rewards white students and staff with unearned privileges and protection.

I am a recipient of those unearned privileges.

I was reminded of this fact by a colleague two summers ago during a professional development that my students and I were giving in Eastern Washington. After our presentation, she raised her hand and said, "I wonder what I could do for my students if I were white."

I am grateful to her, and I now always begin explanations of my work with acknowledgement of my privilege. I self-identify as white, middle class, heterosexual, and cis-gendered, all of which provide me with unearned privileges. I have access to choices and resources that are not distributed evenly in school districts. I am able to be heard by district administrators in a way that is not shared by my colleagues of color. My unearned privileges allow me to move around within our oppressive educational system more easily than some of my colleagues doing similar work.

Acknowledging privilege is important, as Brianna demonstrates on page 30 where she says, "I have had a privileged life. My family are fair-skinned people, even the braceros. ...I want to use my privilege to help others that don't have it." Like Brianna, I also want to acknowledge my privilege and use it to help end systems of oppression. The students in this book have powerful voices and powerful stories. My goal is to create spaces where people will listen, so the students feel heard and oppressive systems begin to break down.

I strive to be a revolutionary.

Storytelling

In my twelve years as the Migrant Graduation Specialist (MGS) for the Mount Vernon School District, I have experimented with a myriad of strategies to engage migrant students in school, and by far the best strategy I have found is personal storytelling.

Through the students' writings in this book, it is clear that many suffer from chronic trauma due to ongoing exposure to factors such as stress, fear, instability, violence, neglect, and oppression.

Unfortunately, chronic trauma often negatively affects students' ability to learn in school. Children who have experienced chronic trauma might struggle with focusing and learning, forming relationships with teachers, self-regulation, negative thinking, and hypervigilance, all of which can lead to absenteeism, disengagement, and ultimately educational failure.

The good news is that children can heal from chronic trauma. The best combination of recognized methods I have found for facilitating this healing from chronic trauma includes:

- A consistent, caring adult
- Peer support
- Trauma-informed personal storytelling

I created the Migrant Leaders Club ten years ago as a safe place for students to begin to engage in school. Today, we use club time to focus on storytelling because it has had such positive results for the students.

Storytelling starts slowly in our weekly club meetings. Middle school students start each meeting by creating a circle of chairs. Then they draw a thermometer on the white board where students can share how they're feeling by adding their name— high on the thermometer if they are feeling good, low if they are feeling bad. I encourage students to share how they're feeling with the group, if desired.

After a student shares, I repeat the themes the student touched on (for example, worry about grades, arguments at home, or sibling problems) and ask the other students to raise their hand if they can relate to those themes. This is a great way for club members to begin to share bits of their story with the group, without having to actually speak.

Next, we address any club business we have to discuss (upcoming projects, field trips, or new opportunities). All club activities come directly from student interests. I present potential opportunities, and the students decide which to pursue. Nothing happens in club without full student buy-in.

After club business, we play games, do team-building activities, or share stories. Our favorite games include Titanic, Human Knot, and Three on a Couch. These games get the students moving and acting a bit silly with each other, which helps with trust building.

Another favorite activity is the Continuum. Students line up shoulder to shoulder facing me so I can see everyone easily. I ask questions, and the students move to the correct spot on the continuum line based on their answer—for example, "How many people live in your home?" The students talk to one another and put themselves in order from low to high. Sometimes I use variations, where students can't speak, or they have to keep both feet on a line of tape on the floor as they move.

I like to increase the intensity of the activity over time. As trust builds during the year, my questions become more personal—for example, "How old were you when you started working the fields?" "On a scale of 1 to 10, how likely are you to graduate from high school?" "How many times have you thought about suicide?" Students can always pass if the question feels too personal. Students often suggest questions as well. This activity allows me to identify specific risk factors among the students and provides them with a safe way to share elements of their story.

Sharing Their Stories with the World

The students' stories move from oral storytelling to print in one of two ways. Students write independently, or they tell me about their life while I type every word they say. In combination with editing and support from our partner, Underground Writing, both methods produce the beautiful writings that you see in this book.

Once students begin to share their stories in club, or with me privately, there is a typical storytelling progression. Students are offered the opportunity to present their stories at small, safe, local events, such as college classes or community meetings. For those students who are not ready for public speaking, we explore storytelling through photography, journalism, acting, video, music, art, radio, and digital storytelling.

Next, they are offered opportunities to present to the larger community, often by showcasing their story at a local theater in our club's spring showcase, *The Hidden Truth*. Once students consider themselves experienced storytellers or public speakers, usually starting in the eighth grade, they are invited to travel to speaking engagements.

Each new travel opportunity couples students who have not previously traveled with students who are veterans to promote natural peer mentoring. Audiences frequently respond with standing ovations. The students are awe-struck by their ability to influence educators, professionals, and lawmakers, while also inspiring other youth.

The healing and hope that migrant students receive through these trips and speaking engagements has increased their confidence, which has led directly to their staying in school. I estimate that our club's high school graduation rate is approximately 90 percent, much higher than our state's migrant graduation rate of 68 percent.

In Mount Vernon, this model is working, and while I want to celebrate that success, I'm nagged by a sense that it's not enough. Part of my students' trauma comes from having to navigate daily an educational system that sees them as lacking. While we help them to process their trauma, we must simultaneously fight to dismantle this trauma-inducing oppressive educational system.

Our students are fighting every day for their right to an education. They deserve revolutionary educators who are willing to fight alongside them.

Janice Blackmore
Founder and Advisor | Mount Vernon Migrant Leaders Club
Migrant Graduation Specialist | Mount Vernon School District
janiceblackmore@gmail.com

Credits

In Underground Writing creative writing workshops, teachers always begin by sharing works of literature—works by writers as distant as Homer and Shakespeare and as near as recently published young-adult novels and poetry.

The quotations in this anthology represent some of the many writers who have inspired these middle school and high school students to, as Juan Felipe Herrera puts it in the Foreword, "ink and splash" their stories onto these pages—to join the on-going conversation that is literature.

Selected Bibliography

Allende, Isabel. Author of novels including *The House of Spirits* and *Daughter of Fortune*. Quoted from BrainyQuote.com (https://www.brainyquote.com/quotes/isabel_allende_466138).

Angelou, Maya (1969). *I Know Why the Caged Bird Sings*. Random House. Quoted from BrainyQuote.com (https://www.brainyquote.com/quotes/maya_angelou_133956).

Esquivel, Laura (1992). Carol and Thomas Christiansen, trans. *Like Water for Chocolate*. Doubleday.

Herrera, Juan Felipe (2015). *Notes on the Assemblage*. City Lights Publishers.

Hudes, Quiara Alegría, book and lyrics. Erin McKeown, music and lyrics. *Miss You Like Hell*. (2018). Theatre Communications Group.

Ledesma, Ramón Mesa (2013). *Migrant Sun*. Village Books. See www.migrantsun.com.

L'Engle, Madeline. Author of *A Wrinkle in Time*. Quoted from Goodreads.com (https://www.goodreads.com/quotes/5193-a-book-too-can-be-a-star-a-living-fire).

Neruda, Pablo (2005). Ilan Stavans, ed. *The Poetry of Pablo Neruda*. Farrar, Strauss and Giroux. Quoted from Azquotes.com (https://www.azquotes.com/author/10743-Pablo_Neruda/tag/dream).

Index

237